What the Reviewers Say

"*The Mt. Shasta Book* demonstrates that it's more than a straightforward guide to Shasta's skiing and trekking routes...Selters and Zanger offer sound advice on avoiding hazards while never sounding preachy. Instead, they give the common-sense approaches that will put you in touch with the strange, almost mystical beauty of the mountain while telling you the smart ways to avoid the peak when the complexities of weather or terrain make it dangerous...Well worth the cover price."
—Powder Magazine

"...a model guide...excellent topographic map...In addition to detailed trail information, the book provides a good overview of the mountain's geology, flora and fauna. The camping crowd will find this volume indispensable."
—San Francisco Chronicle

"...an exhaustive guide to the hiking trails and climbing routes on this massive volcano...[the] map is excellent."
—The Climbing Art

THE MT. SHASTA BOOK

A Guide to Hiking, Climbing, Skiing,
and Exploring the Mountain
and Surrounding Area

Andy Selters
Michael Zanger

 **Wilderness Press**
BERKELEY

FIRST EDITION August 1989
Second printing August 1990
Third printing August 1992

Cover photography by Kevin Lahey
All other photographs by the authors
Topographic maps by Andy Selters
Photo-maps by Michael Zanger
Cover design by Larry Van Dyke
Book design by Thomas Winnett and Roslyn Bullas

Library of Congress Card Catalog Number 89-40028
International Standard Book Number 0-89997-101-6

Manufactured in the United States of America

Published by Wilderness Press
          2440 Bancroft Way
          Berkeley, CA 94704
          (510) 843-8080
Write for free catalog

Library of Congress Cataloging in Publication Data

Selters, Andrew.
    The Mt. Shasta Book / Andy Selters, Michael Zanger.
        p. cm.
    Includesl index.
    ISBN 0-89997-101-6
    1. Shasta, Mount (Calif.)--Description and travel--Guide-books. 2. Mount
Shasta Wilderness (Calif.)--Description and travel--Guide-books. 3. Moun-
taineering--California--Shasta, Mount--Guide-books. 4. Mountaineering--Califor-
nia--Mount Shasta Wilderness--Guide-books. 5. Natural
history--California--Shasta, Mount--Guide-books. 6. Natural history--California--
Mount Shasta Wilderness--Guide-books. I. Zanger, Michael, 1941- . II. Title.
III. Title: Mount Shasta book.
    F868.S6S45 1989
    917.94'21--dc20   89-40028
                                                            CIP

Contents

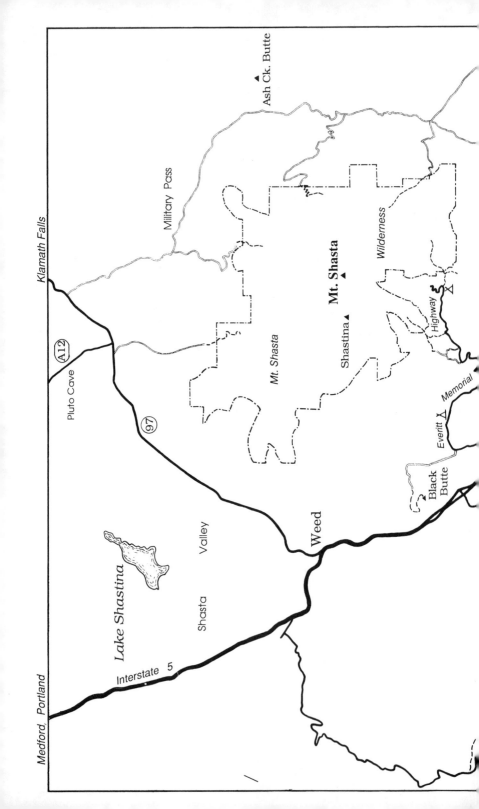

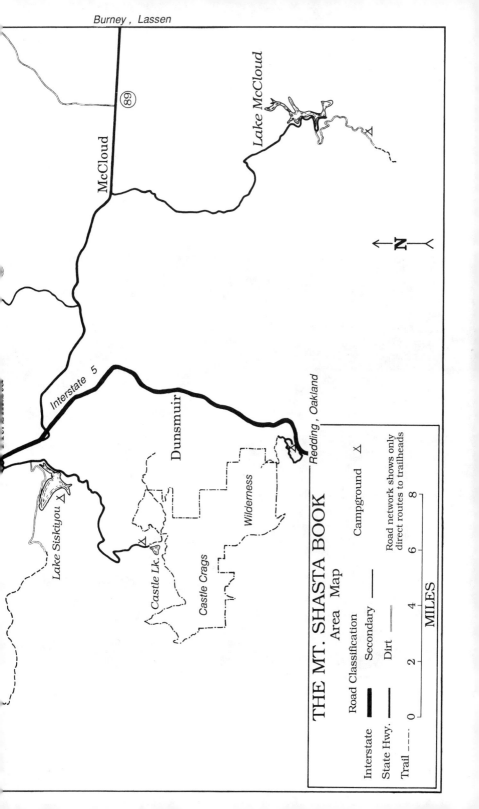

Clearing storm on Mt. Shasta

1 Introduction

Rising to over 10,000 feet above its surroundings, Mt. Shasta appears from a distance almost as an apparition, seemingly too huge to be real. The mountain's overwhelming presence makes Joaquin Miller's surreal description, "lonely as God and white as a winter moon," ring as aptly today as it did a century ago. But Mt. Shasta is a very real eminence, not only inspiring the artist and the mystic in us, but offering some of California's most diverse mountain recreation.

From quiet forests and humming glades, to creaking glaciers and windswept parapets, Shasta's slopes set a magnificent stage for excursions ranging from casual rambles to committing challenges. On many given days one can choose between discovering wildflowers while on a forest trail, taking ice ax and crampons up to the towering summit, clamping on skis to glide over meadows or swish down a high basin, or jumping on a mountain bike to ride over miles of mountain roads.

The core of this book is a practical guide to this wide range of activities. Although, of course, we encourage anyone with an interest to try any and all of them, each excursion requires its own level of expertise, and readers must judge for themselves what they are ready for, and also judge what the conditions and the weather will allow. At one end of the spectrum, the easier hikes require little more than comfortable footgear and common sense. At the other end, the climbing and ski-mountaineering routes require stamina, technical skill and equipment, and a great sensitivity to the mountain's condition and to oneself. For climbers and skiers without experience on a high mountain like Shasta, this book is no substitute for getting instruction and experience on lesser mountains, where endurance,

1

skill and judgment are less critical. In addition to describing the hikes, climbing routes and ski terrain on Shasta, we've described a number of hikes in the surrounding area, and we also suggest some mountain biking routes.

In this book we also introduce Mt. Shasta's geology, flora and fauna. This is because, to us, enjoying activities is only half of "going to the mountains"; the other, more reflective half is coming to know the patterns and processes of the mountain environment. Ideally, during activities and adventures we learn about the environment, and, conversely, while seeking to understand the environment we find adventure and exercise. The two approaches can feed on and balance each other and build more complete experiences and understanding.

However we mountain lovers try to define our interest, though, most of us find that there's more to Mt. Shasta than we can explain. Something overwhelming but not quite tangible draws people to this giant of a mountain. If you approach those who have gone back to Shasta innumerable times—the geologists and the botanists, the climbers and the skiers—and ask them what beside their pastimes they like about Shasta, you'll probably get a rambling affirmation that indeed the mountain is "beautiful" or "impressive"—that indeed they just like to spend time on it. While we can't hope to guide readers into ineffable states of mind, we can hint that for many people Mt. Shasta embodies an inspiring and magical presence, yet a presence probably different for each person who senses it.

Finally, we feel that our responsibility is not only to guide hikers and climbers through their excursions, but to encourage them to leave as little trace of their passing as possible. As a rock-and-ice edifice, Mt. Shasta may be invulnerable, but the mountain's thin, dry soils and high, sterile campsites can be trashed easily by even just one careless visitor. However, when the goal of minimum impact is honored, simple common sense gives rise to the proper careful practices. Perhaps the most important thing this book can do is to stimulate a more sensitive appreciation for the wonder that is Mt. Shasta. Then Shasta—a bold, attention-getting statement from the natural world—can help us all develop a greater appreciation of and care for the natural world in general.

2 Weather

Mt. Shasta is known world-wide for its towering lenticular clouds—those lens-shaped giants that park over the summit like a galactic stack of pancakes. Shasta's winds are also legendary, and during prolonged winter storms aircraft give the mountain a wide berth while climbers and skiers stay indoors. In the summer, billowing cumulus thunderheads can form quickly during afternoons, sometimes producing thunderstorms before sundown.

Nearly all of us who have hiked, camped or climbed have heard the expression, "Mountains make their own weather." In a sense, this is true. But in reality, mountains—and Mt. Shasta is a prime example—are simply showing weather changes *earlier* than the surrounding lowlands.

Certain weather signs on Mt. Shasta give us clues to approaching weather changes and storms. Storms usually move into the Shasta area from the southwest. The first indication of an approaching storm is a change in the wind direction from the prevailing north or east wind to a southwest wind. Wind speed is also likely to increase. Another sign of an approaching storm is the moisture content of the air as indicated by the formation of clouds. The leading edge of a storm usually shows high clouds—cirrus and cirrostratus. These high clouds thicken and lower as the storm nears. Low level moisture is indicated by Mt. Shasta's famous lenticular, and other less defined cap clouds. Before storm clouds completely cover the sky, the top of Mt. Shasta will usually be covered by a thick cap cloud, which will descend as the storm approaches. Temperatures may be relatively warm before the cap cloud forms but will fall dramatically once it is in place.

Many hours—or only a few—may elapse from the time a storm's leading edge reaches Shasta until low clouds collect and precipitation

3

Shasta and lenticular clouds, from the north

begins. If towering cumulus clouds are visible as the storm approaches, the time will usually be short, and thunderstorms may occur with gusty winds, lightning, hail and other associated severe weather.

If you're climbing or hiking on Mt. Shasta below a cap cloud, observing the cloud's actions can be very helpful in forecasting weather changes: If the cap stays above 12,000 feet, the storm *may* not get worse. Winds will remain high, but the cap cloud may even begin to diminish. If the cap cloud thickens and descends, the storm will probably worsen and descent from the mountain is advisable. When a storm forms quickly, such as an afternoon thunderstorm, its duration is usually brief—sometimes only a few hours. But if a storm takes one or more days to develop, it can often last for several days before dissipating.

The latest weather information for the Shasta area is available from the following sources:

National Weather Service 24-hour recorded message: (916) 221-5613

The Fifth Season outdoor shop 24-hour climbing report: (916) 926-5555

3 Hiking

On Shasta

Mt. Shasta has a reputation of not offering much to the hiker, but actually there's a lot to choose from. This reputation arose largely because there are fewer than 10 miles of constructed trails on the mountain. But in addition to these trails, hikers' boots have beaten a number of quite evident "trails of use" to popular destinations, and some abandoned, partly overgrown jeep roads offer scenic, isolated hiking. For those who want to leave the trail, Shasta's open vegetation allows pleasant cross-country hiking and fairly easy route finding, so in this book we suggest a few off-trail excursions.

The mountains near Mt. Shasta offer some excellent hiking also, with grand panoramas of The Mountain. In the latter part of this chapter we describe some of the better known of these hikes, all of which can be done in a day from a base at Mount Shasta city.

In nearly all the hikes described here, you retrace your steps back to the trailhead. The mileages given are total for the hikes.

As of this writing (May, 1990), no permit is required to enter the Mt. Shasta Wilderness. The U.S. Forest Service anticipates completion of their Mt. Shasta Wilderness Management Plan by late summer of 1990. They then plan to issue permits on a trial basis through 1991. After that, they *may* decide to implement quotas.

Trailheads

In many of the trailhead descriptions, a mileage in **boldface** type gives the distance from the previous boldface mileage or from the start. Thus the boldface mileages are a noncumulative log. For example, "...after **1.2** miles turn left (W) and drive up a couple...after **1.7**

5

miles turn..." means that the second turn is 1.7 miles after the first. Mileages in normal type provide additional information.

Much of the access to Mt. Shasta is from Everitt Memorial Highway, which leads from Mount Shasta city up to timberline on the south flank of the mountain. To get to the highway, from North Mt. Shasta Blvd. turn east onto Alma St. and continue for 0.3 mile, past a gradual right turn, to the start of the highway.

Getting to trailheads on the north and east sides of Mt. Shasta involves somewhat tedious and rough driving through a network of logging roads, but ordinary passenger vehicles can get to any of the trailheads described here. The descriptions cover every junction. Although logging activity has declined in recent years, new logging roads occasionally change the road network on the north and east sides of the mountain. Some of the Forest Service's signs for routes to trailheads are misleading or outdated, and some of the signs have been vandalized, but the descriptions here were accurate as of the spring of 1990.

Horse Camp (from Bunny Flat)
3.4 miles round trip

The best-known trail on Shasta, this path takes you to the timberline cabin owned by the Sierra Club Foundation. Anyone may visit the cabin and use its library. With Shasta rising directly above it and a fountain of pure spring water beside it, Horse Camp lures many hikers to stay overnight at one of the established camp spots there.

Sierra Club Alpine Lodge at Horse Camp

Trailhead

There are two trails to Horse Camp off Everitt Highway, from Bunny Flat and from Sand Flat. More people take the trail from Bunny Flat, although it is about 0.1 miles longer, because it climbs more gradually, starting 100 feet higher. From the town of Mount Shasta, Bunny Flat is 10.9 miles up Everitt Highway, and the trailhead is right on the road. There are a large parking area and an outhouse here.

Description

With a full view of Mt. Shasta, we start north along the west edge of an expansive dry meadow. We then promptly turn west over a small ridge and hike northwest through more-open areas of Bloomer's goldbush, on the fringes of Shasta red-fir forest. The wide trail (an old road for the first ³/₄ mile) jogs north, then continues climbing gently to a broad, open ravine where young red firs lie strewn about. These trees are the most recent victims of the large snow avalanches that roar down Avalanche Gulch during unusually heavy winters.

From this ravine our trail turns northwest up the side of a forested ridge, to reach the trail coming up from Sand Flat. This latter trail has pretty much followed this ridge from the forested trailhead, climbing through a manzanita clearing with logging stumps and then through forest again to this junction.

Now we hike on a steady grade northeast along the flank of the ridge, pausing perhaps to hear the twitters and calls of mountain chickadees and Steller jays. At the end of the climb a jog northwest heralds our arrival at the meadows of Horse Camp. Here the Sierra Club posts a summer caretaker, who can answer questions about everything from climbing conditions to the cabin's history, from the latest local environmental controversy to where it's best to camp. If you do camp here, we strongly recommend that you use a stove, and if you must build a fire please be frugal with wood. Camping is allowed inside the cabin only in emergencies.

Horse Camp is so named because it was here that early-day climbers tethered their horses while ascending Shasta. Above Horse Camp the fir forest gives way to open timberline slopes, luring hikers farther. Behind the cabin the Olberman's Causeway starts climbers up the traditional summit climbing route, and this path makes a nice extension for hikers to follow a way as well.

Side trips

For those interested in some cross-country hiking, two particularly scenic destinations from here are Hidden Valley and Green Butte.

"Krummholz" whitebark pines in Hidden Valley

Hidden Valley is a broad, perched bench in Cascade Gulch that makes an excellent place from which to look south over seemingly all of California. From the Sierra Club lodge, look almost due north along the left skyline of Shasta and you'll see a small but striking finger of rock. This pinnacle, Point 9487 on the topo map, lies directly above and south of Hidden Valley. Strike off toward the pinnacle and then climb up sandy, forested slopes to a tiny basin. Continue north, climbing past a few outstanding tall firs and up more sandy slopes, to eventually turn into the drainage of Cascade Gulch. The final stretch to Hidden Valley is an exasperating traversing climb up a rocky slope to the head of the gulch. But in Hidden Valley you're rewarded with a reliable stream in a *krummholz* "forest," where Shasta and Shastina loom over you in an amphitheater of high mountain grandeur.

Green Butte is almost due east of Horse Camp, and from its summit you can also look far to the south, with rugged Sargents Ridge towering behind you. At this writing, however, there is a proposal to level off the top of the butte and build a ski lift to the leveled summit.

From Horse Camp hike east across the sandy, open drainage of Avalanche Gulch and then start climbing steadily, aiming for the broad, relatively gentle slope in the major ridge to the east. This slope, called an erosion surface, was smoothed by gradual erosion; it escaped the cutting of long-ago glaciers on either side. From this broad slope, hike northeast to near the summit of Point 9365, then turn southeast to descend along the very narrow rock ridge to the summit of Green Butte, so named for its distinctively green rock. Many of the summit rocks are *fulgurites*, rocks fused into glassiness by lightning.

Gray Butte
2.8 miles round trip

This hike takes you through meadow and forest to the panoramic crest of one of Shasta's satellite buttes.

Trailhead

Drive up Everitt Highway 11.4 miles and turn into the Panther Meadow campground. Keep left at a couple of campground spurs and park at the east edge of the campground, just below the highway.

Description

Our trail starts east across Panther Meadow, a rich, verdant glade unusual on Mt. Shasta. Particularly strong springs above the meadow keep the ground here saturated, preventing tree growth but providing

Shasta from Panther Meadow. Green Butte on left, Ski Bowl in center, Sargents Ridge at right.

a rich substrate for subalpine herbs. Different degrees of saturation here favor different plants: the wettest areas adjacent to stream channels are dense with rushes, monkey flowers and swamp onions; most of the meadow is seasonally saturated and dominated by heather, bilberry and laurel; the meadow's drier periphery supports goldenbush and Shasta arnica, although one can see that young mountain hemlocks and Shasta red-firs are starting to claim the drier ground. This meadow vegetation is fragile, so please stay on the trail as you cross.

Across the   meadow we duck into Shasta red-fir forest and gradually climb on a rocky, dusty track. We continue east along the south base of an unnamed butte, winding our way up to a saddle where a few whitebark pines mix with the firs. Here, 0.6 mile from Panther Meadow campground, an unsigned trail heads northeast for upper Squaw Valley, while ours leads south and starts a steadily climbing traverse along the east slope of Gray Butte.

As we climb the steady grade, views open up to Red Butte and the flanks of Mt. Shasta. Before long we turn west around the east ridge of Gray Butte, stepping from a thicket of young mountain hemlocks into a mature forest of husky adult trees, perhaps the finest mature hemlock stand in the Shasta area.

We continue a steady climb under the hemlocks, passing pinemat manzanita and violets as we arc around the southeast slopes of Gray Butte and gradually approach a dirt road that serves radio facilities atop the butte. We arrive at the open crest of the butte with a panorama across Strawberry Valley to Mt. Eddy and the rest of the Siskiyous and the Trinity Alps. More to the south we see Castle Crags, and beyond the McCloud River country rises Lassen Peak. For full views of Mt. Shasta, you might want to hike northeast up the ridge to Gray Butte's highest point.

Squaw Valley
4.4 miles round trip

Lush green meadows framed by groves of delicate mountain hemlock make Squaw Valley—Shasta's only extensive verdant drainage—one of the mountain's most popular destinations. Although the Forest Service has never constructed a trail here, except for a couple of short sections the track is quite evident. Many people enjoy meeting up with this *de facto* trail after a cross-country loop around Red Butte.

Trailhead

Our trail branches off the previously described Gray Butte Trail, which starts at Panther Meadow. Many people, however, shorten the hike by starting from the old Ski Bowl lot at the end of Everitt Highway, then hiking cross-country over the saddle north of Point 8332 to meet the trail in the open flats south of The Gate, a rocky defile.

Description

From Panther Meadow we take the Gray Butte Trail east for 0.6 mile to a saddle north of Gray Butte. Here the Gray Butte Trail turns south, while our path contours northeast for a short distance. Soon afterward we rise over a steep, rocky ridgelet, then climb a bit more along the east base of that ridgelet. Next we follow the path on a narrow way through shrubby mountain hemlocks, curving northeast to some slabs that look east to nearby Red Butte.

From these slabs we wind northeast, crossing a ravine and heading toward broad, open flats below the west walls of Red Butte. The path disintegrates in the dark, loose ash in these flats, but by keeping on a north-northeast bearing we work toward the head of the shallow drainage. This stark, silent basin supports a few austere forbs like knotweed and buckwheat, and numerous windflowers nodding their white blossoms over the dark sand only add to the surreal aura.

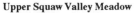

Upper Squaw Valley Meadow

Near the head of the shallow drainage we find trail again and walk through The Gate. A short, steep drop then takes us into the canyon between Red Butte and Sargents Ridge. Now our trail steadily descends into hemlock country, keeping north above the rocky canyon floor. Before long the track turns northeast through a hemlock grove to a stream. We cross another fork or two of the stream and then climb a short way to arrive at upper Squaw Valley Meadow.

Here sedges, heather and various wildflowers grown in a rich carpet beside a perennial brook, fed by a spring that issues from the snowy ramparts of Shasta above. Unlike most drainages on Shasta, the substrate underlying Squaw Valley Creek somehow keeps a steady flow of water running, and "stringer" meadows like this one lie beside the creek well into the forest belt. These meadows—so precious on Shasta—are easily trampled into mud, so please refrain from hiking on them. Some of Shasta's religious groups particularly enjoy these meadows, but unfortunately they often leave stones arranged in words of testimony to their religious experience.

Red Butte Loop Variation
(Cross Country)

The trail to Squaw Valley runs around the north side of Red Butte. In order to form a loop, many hikers enjoy going around the south side of the butte, returning on the north side trail.

From the saddle on the Gray Butte Trail (0.6 mile from Panther Meadow), where the trail to Squaw Valley forks northeast, you'll want to eye the basin to the southeast, and plot your course, which will cross the basin below you and climb back up to a prominent bench on the south side of Red Butte. With that bench in mind, strike off east, heading down into fir-and-hemlock forest and reaching a creek before long at the bottom of the basin.

You'll probably want to head down the basin a short way before starting a steady climb east toward the bench. Stay fairly close to the southern abutments of Red Butte, however, where relatively moderate slopes readily allow you to climb due east. When you arrive at the bench, you break into an expansive, sparsely vegetated meadow, a secluded world of its own. At the meadow's southeast edge a small lake of pooled snowmelt remains into early summer.

Hike northeast across the bench, back into a forest edge, and come to a precipitous dropoff. Without getting too close, head northwest along the top of the cliff and past its far end, and you'll see a worn path traversing down into a ravine. Follow this path as it traverses the gravelly slope of a small cinder cone, and climb out the other side of the ravine to then contour north. Descending slightly as you traverse north, you'll eventually come to a meadow where a feeder of Squaw Valley Creek keeps the ground soggy year-round.

Here you turn northwest to climb along the southern edge of the meadow, keeping near the talus at the northeast base of Red Butte. Your climb steepens as you re-enter forest and pass the spring that wets the meadow. After a steady climb you reach the rocky canyon between Red Butte and Sargents Ridge, and you can pick up the trail to upper Squaw Valley. By following it west through The Gate, you can return to the Gray Butte Trail and Panther Meadow.

Clear Creek

4.0 miles round trip

Although the route to this trailhead is complex, and the initial stretch of trail is a mess, this hike takes you along the rim of spectacular Mud Creek Canyon to timberline views dominated by Shasta and its four eastern glaciers.

Trailhead

From McCloud take Highway 89 east 3.0 miles and turn left (N) on paved Pilgrim Creek Road. Follow this road as it curves northeast, and after 5.3 miles turn left (NW) onto Road 41N15. Go northwest on this road **5.0** miles, to where it intersects Road 31. Continue straight across Road 31, ignoring spurs which lead off to the right (N) after 0.1, 0.5, and 0.7 miles, respectively. The last spur road is a previous trailhead-access road rendered unusable from recent logging. Follow a 180 degree right-hand switchback at 1.5 miles from Road 31, and pass a connecting spur on the right at 2.2 miles. Continue straight, ignoring additional spurs to the left at 2.3 and 2.5 miles, and another pair of tracks leading right at 2.7 and 2.8 miles. Continue to a trailhead parking area at road's end, **3.0** miles from the intersection with Road 31.

Recent logging (1989) has taken its toll on the last 3 miles of road; eroded sections may prove difficult for passenger cars, and a maze of logging roads marked with colored ribbons can be confusing. Until

Looking up Mud Creek Canyon

the U.S. Forest Service upgrades the road, passenger cars should carry a shovel.

Description

The Clear Creek "trail" is actually an old jeep road that evolved from use by 4WD enthusiasts and woodcutters. Since the creation of Mt. Shasta Wilderness, the Forest Service has blocked the trail with a gate and multiple ditches and slashpiles to keep off-road vehicles from entering the wilderness. The best way to reach the easy hiking above the troublesome blockades is to surmount the roadcut at road's end and embark cross-country northwest, keeping close to the rim of the canyon. This way you hike cross-country through open red-fir forest, negotiating only an occasional deadfall instead of the numerous blockades in the "trail" a couple of hundred yards east.

After ½ mile of cross-country walking you'll be past the blockades and you'll come across the old jeep track, which runs just east of the canyon rim. As you reach about 7000 feet elevation, the forest opens up into groves that allow views of Shasta and Mud Creek Canyon. Along Shasta's skyline you see Shastarama Point and Thumb Rock above the Konwakiton Glacier; on Shasta's eastern flank you see the Watkins and Wintun glaciers; and in the depths of Mud Creek Canyon you see a couple of spectacular waterfalls.

Mud Creek Canyon is Shasta's largest and oldest canyon, dating from the proto-Mt. Shasta of a few hundred thousand years ago. Glaciers have at various times filled the canyon, largely excavating it to its grand depths. Outburst floods and general stream action have also scoured the unstable canyon walls.

Our trail continues on a rollercoaster course along the east rim of the canyon. As we climb in the area above the confluence of Clear Creek and Mud Creek far below, the firs thin and whitebark pines enter the scene. We continue climbing into the whitebark's realm, where Clark nutcrackers squawk at our intrusion into their domain. You can follow the track into the *krummholz* zone, to near 8300 feet. At this height Clear Creek's drainage broadens and allows one to traverse west ¼ mile to a surprisingly verdant destination, the source springs of Clear Creek.

Brewer Creek
4.0 miles round trip

Constructed in 1986, this trail offers well-graded access to timberline on Shasta's relatively unvisited east slopes. Although the drive to the trailhead is fairly complex, the roads are quite smooth and reasonably well signed. The hike rewards one with pleasant walking among whitebark-pine parklands, good views of Shasta and its glaciers, and access to summer ski slopes.

Trailhead

Allow 2 hours from the city of Mount Shasta. Take Highway 89 east through McCloud. Three miles from McCloud turn left (N) on Pilgrim Creek Road, which is paved for a distance. Continue on this, the main road, as it turns northeast, for **5.2** miles. Here, turn left (NW) onto Road 41N15 and continue straight past many spur roads **5.0** miles to an intersection with Road 31. Turn right (N) onto Road 31 and (ignoring an old BREWER CREEK sign pointing west at about mile 4) continue **6.0** miles to turn left (N) onto Road 19. After a very short distance turn left (W) onto Road 42N02 and follow it northwest **2.8** miles to Road 42N10. Turn left (SW) onto Road 42N10 and keep right on it at a junction 1.1 miles later. Follow Road 42N10 up two switchbacks to the trailhead, **3.1** miles from Road 42N02.

Description

We start hiking south, climbing up an old roadbed. Where the old road switchbacks, the trail continues south, and then it turns west to regain the road and turn south again. Half a mile from the trailhead the road ends for good, and we start a series of long, lazy switchbacks that take us from an open red-fir forest into a parkland of whitebark pines. Hardy wildflowers that dot the ashy soil between whitebarks include violets, phlox and Shasta knotweed.

After several switchbacks our trail takes a fairly steady course south, still gradually climbing through extensive stands of burly whitebarks. Now, however, we get full views of Shasta, including the Wintun and Hotlum glaciers. The track crosses a few dry ravines, then comes to the fairly reliable flows of Brewer Creek. Snow will provide a bridge across this creek until at least early July, although take care that such a bridge is thick enough.

From Brewer Creek the trail contours south $^1/_4$ mile to meet an old jeep road. Built illegally by 4WD enthusiasts, this road is traceable west to 8300 feet, and beyond where it fades out skiers can find summer snow to schuss on, typically into August. If you follow the road downhill (E) $^1/_8$ mile you come to a fork. The southbound branch curves to the top of a small, sandy ridge, and from there heads uphill southwest and west, continuing for another 1 $^1/_2$ sandy miles to over 9000 feet, petering out among the highest, most dwarfed *krummholz* whitebarks.

Ash Creek Falls (Cross-Country)

From the Brewer Creek Trail an experienced hiker can trek to Ash Creek Falls, Shasta's prettiest waterfall. The 2 1/2-mile round trip from the Brewer Creek Trail requires some cross-country route finding and scrambling. From the old jeep road atop the sandy ridge mentioned above, contour south and drop into a large, dry ravine. Climb back out of the ravine and contour around the next ridge at the 7800 foot level. Curve west at that contour, and you'll soon pass beside a dropoff from where the falls are partly visible. The best views are to be had from across the canyon, however, and to reach them you'll have to angle down to cross the stream above the falls. Take extreme care to find the easiest way down this slope; if you are on route, only a very short cliff near the bottom will require some scrambling. Through late summer, deep snow forms a sturdy, convenient bridge over the creek, and once across you can reach viewpoints by climbing directly upslope through a band of whitebarks.

North Gate

Climbers heading up to the Hotlum and Bolam glacier routes have developed this trail, and it's not hard to follow for 1.6 miles up into the whitebark-pine zone. From there one can wander up any number of knolls and moraines to win encompassing views of Shasta and the country north.

Trailhead

Access is quite complex and rough; follow these directions carefully and allow 1 1/2 hours from Weed. From Weed's only stoplight drive north on Highway 97 12.8 miles to Military Pass Road. Turn right (SE) at the historical marker here and continue on this fairly rough "main" road. Cross under railroad tracks, and 4.7 miles from Highway 97 keep left, avoiding Andesite Road. Our road (occasionally signed as Road 19) curves and continues generally southeast for another 2.4 miles to a major junction at Military Pass. Turn right here, where in 1988 a NORTH GATE sign pointed south up Road 42N76. From here, the drive goes through a maze of rough logging roads, best described in noncumulative log style:

> **0.2** Keep straight (S)
> **0.6** Curve right (W) onto Road 42N16
> **0.9** Keep straight (W)

0.8 Curve SW and then turn left (S) onto Road 42N16
0.3 At a triple junction turn right (SW) to go uphill onto
Road 42N16
0.8 Keep left around a sweeping 180° curve along the edge
of a clearcut.

Continue east through the clearcut as far as your vehicle can easily
go. Those with passenger cars will have to park in the clearcut and
hike up the road to the trailhead; those with high-clearance vehicles
will be able to turn south and climb another **0.4** mile through uncut
forest to the trailhead at nearly 7300 feet.

Description

Our trail starts off in prime Shasta red-fir forest, climbing steadily
south. At ⅛ mile from the trailhead, the track is a bit hard to follow,
but continuing uphill south-southwest near the eastern base of the
dacite dome above keeps us on route. The track quickly becomes
distinct again, and we follow it through some brief turns and gradual
switchbacks, heading generally southwest.

Before long our path steepens up a ravine, and soon thereafter
enters the realm of whitebark pines. Here grow some of the most
magnificent whitebarks anywhere—stout, proud trees that nevertheless show the golden wood where the elements killed the growing
tissue. Some of these trees rival the largest whitebark officially

Hiking through whitebark pines near North Gate

measured, in Grand Teton National Park. Our trail continues southwest into a sandy basin between two hills, disappearing into sand at about 8200 feet. To get views of nearby Shasta and the distant valleys and mountains to the north, hike up either hill. Climbers will want to continue southwest past Point 8852 and beyond the next basin, as described in the climbing chapter.

When returning to your vehicle, be alert for the indistinct section of the trail 1/8 mile above the trailhead. Here, many people happen onto another path that heads northeast to other logging roads and a "trailhead" that the Forest Service has signed INCONSTANCE TRAILHEAD . To avoid that path, as you near the North Gate trailhead, keep very near the east base of the steep dacite dome to the west, and as you pass it veer north to your vehicle.

Whitney Falls
3.4 miles round trip

This casual hike takes you to a good viewpoint 1/3 mile from Whitney Falls, a freefall of about 250 feet. Although most of the hike follows an abandoned jeep trail, open scenery and solitude make it a pleasant excursion. During midsummer this sunny trail can be baking hot.

Trailhead

From the Weed stoplight drive north on Highway 97 10.3 miles to unsigned Bolam Road. If you come to paved County Road A12, which branches north, you've gone 0.3 mile too far on Highway 97. On fairly good quality Bolam Road, keep driving south, avoiding an eastbound (left) road at **0.2** mile from Highway 97 and another **0.8** mile farther. Another **0.5** mile farther, continue straight across railroad tracks and maintain a southbound course past a couple of other forks to reach the trailhead, 3.8 miles from Highway 97.

Description

Begin by crossing Bolam Creek's dry wash just west of the trailhead, and then turn south onto the jeep road on the west side of this shallow drainage. Phlox, sulfur flower and paintbrush dot this sandy track, and scattered Jeffrey pines, antelope brush and mountain mahogany thinly cover the surrounding hills. Half a mile from the trailhead our path switchbacks up out of the drainage into full view of Shasta and the Bolam Glacier, and to the north we see across Shasta Valley to the northern Siskiyous.

Shasta from near Bolam Creek

We continue south along the west rim of Bolam Creek's dry ravine for a way, then bend east to climb a couple of switchbacks. These take us south back across the drainage to a steady climb to another switchback. At this switchback a worn-in trail of use ducks off west into a ravine shaded by a grove of Jeffrey pines and white firs. This path will take us to the Whitney Falls overlook.

From the shaded ravine our trail of use climbs steeply around a small ridge, then turns south a short distance to the brink of the impressively eroded canyon of Whitney Creek. The falls plunge off an overhanging cliff at the head of the canyon, and if you listen carefully you'll hear rocks, gravel and mud clattering over the falls; Whitney Falls is anything but a clear stream, for glacial silt and Shasta's unstable ashy debris readily dissolve into the creek. During recent hot summers the Whitney Glacier has released outburst floods (see the "Geology" Chapter) that have poured over the falls and continued downstream to damage property beyond Highway 97. The loose canyon walls below us show ample evidence of undercutting by these and previous floods.

Circum-Shasta Hike

Hiking around Mt. Shasta is arguably the best way to get to know the mountain. In fact, John Muir wrote:

> "...far better than climbing [Mt. Shasta] is going around its warm fertile base, enjoying its bounties like a bee circling around a bank of flowers.... As you sweep around so grand a centre the mountain itself seems to turn.... One glacier after another comes into view, and the outlines of the mountain are ever changing."

Relatively few people take this ultimate Shasta backpack, partly because it's a fairly committing endeavor, with no trail to follow. In route finding, strenuousness and terrain, it should be considered a moderate but long mountaineering endeavor. Knowing how to self-arrest and carrying an ice ax can be important in early season high around Shastina. Shasta's relatively open slopes help make route finding fairly easy, but soft, ashy underfooting occasionally gets tedious. One needs to plan the hike carefully to camp at water sources, and to find passages across some of the canyons.

With these cautions in mind, confident backpackers who are comfortable with occasional scrambling should not be deterred from taking one of California's finest backcountry hikes. Really fit hikers can complete the route in four days, and five would be comfortable for most hikers.

Different hikers choose to circle the mountain at different elevations. There are many route variations, especially on the mountain's west flanks, but most hikers stay near the 8000 feet treeline. What follows is a general clockwise description of the possibilities, with mention of key canyon crossings and important campsites.

Starting from Horse Camp, some hikers stay low, perhaps planning a first camp at Cascade Gulch or Diller Canyon. In dry years these canyons might not offer water, although you can always count on finding snow to melt in Diller Canyon. An alternative route is to go high and spend the first night in Hidden Valley, where water is always available. This sets you up for a higher traverse around Shastina, over spurs 9363 and 9084. Staying high gives you a wonderfully scenic and somewhat shorter route, but it takes you across a couple of trying scree slopes, and you have to negotiate some short cliff bands, 1/4 mile south of Diller Canyon and about 3/4 miles north of it.

To traverse the Graham Creek-Bolam Creek area, it's best to avoid the morainal hills below the Whitney and Bolam glaciers by either keeping fairly low (but above Coquette Falls) or going fairly high, across the terminus of the Whitney glacier. For those who go high, a reliable if dusty camp awaits in the basin below the Bolam Glacier, at about 9600 feet. From this camp it's best to descend along the east side of Bolam Creek to treeline.

In the North Gate vicinity, most hikers contour just south of Point 8852, and gradually lose elevation as they continue east. Another option is to climb over the morainal benches near Point 9535, where there's excellent camping and almost always water. To continue east off these benches, descend a key sandy gully through some cliff bands east-southeast of Point 9535.

Those who are relatively high will find difficulty in crossing Gravel Creek's canyon. The canyon walls consist of steep, unstable ash with boulders perched on it. Members of a party must take special care to avoid knocking rocks onto one another, and not to climb directly below or above one another. Below 7500 feet the canyon walls are safer and not as high.

The next key point is Ash Creek right above the falls. To get there, hike through whitebark parklands near the 8000-foot level across Brewer Creek (reliable and clear). Contour around the ridge just north of the falls at 7800 feet and then cut back west to descend into

At timberline below Avalanche Gulch

the canyon above the falls. An 8-foot cliff on this descent requires some scrambling. Solid snow—avalanche debris—usually offers a convenient bridge across Ash Creek until late in summer. On the south side of the canyon, climb directly upslope through a band of whitebarks.

Cold Creek, Pilgrim Creek and Clear Creek are all reliable and silt-free. Contour around Clear Creek's canyon at about 7800 feet to set up for the crucial crossing of intimidating Mud Creek Canyon. From 7700 feet on the canyon rim, drop straight into the canyon at the uppermost grove of full-size firs, just upcanyon from a bare landslide area. Near the canyon bottom, again take special care to avoid sending rocks onto partners. Cross Mud Creek a couple of hundred yards above the falls, and climb directly up a steep, faint drainage to get back out of the canyon.

From the south rim of the canyon, a course that contours near 7800 feet will take you around Red Fir Ridge to Squaw Valley Creek, from where you can either climb through The Gate or traverse south around Red Butte to Panther Meadow and return to Everitt Highway.

The Planned Trail Around Shasta

The oft-proposed trail around Mt. Shasta is finally in the works. The Mt. Shasta Trail Association hopes to complete a well-graded trail in 5-10 years from this writing. The trail will circle the mountain generally between 6000 feet and 8000 feet, although the exact route has not yet been drawn, pending the Forest Service's final Wilderness Management Plan.

The total budget for the project is $1.5 million, of which the Forest Service is providing less than one third. The nonprofit Mt. Shasta Trail Association is raising the remainder, through membership, donations and merchandise sales. The Association needs volunteers in all capacities, from raising funds to excavating rocks. If you can help, or would like additional information, contact it at P.O. Box 36, Mount Shasta, CA 96067.

Hiking Near Shasta

McCloud River Preserve
5.2 miles round trip

Most of the McCloud River drainage has been logged over, and dams have stilled the river's tumbling waters in its lower and upper reaches. But a major stretch of its inner canyon remains a refuge of wilderness, because Bay Area aristocrats bought the land from Central Pacific Railroad for a retreat. In 1973 they donated their upper holdings to The Nature Conservancy, and now much of this corridor has become a wonderful spot for hikers and, especially, fly fishermen (limited to 10 anglers at one time).

Trailhead

From the town of McCloud, turn south off of Highway 89 at the service station, onto Squaw Valley Road. Continue on this for **9.2** miles, and then keep right near a boat ramp at McCloud Reservoir. After curving for **2.2** miles above the reservoir, veer right at a sharp turn onto a dirt road signed AH-DI-NA. After **0.6** mile keep left, and after another **1.8** miles keep straight, through a junction. Continuing past the spur to Ah-Di-Na Campground, after **4.4** miles stay right. The trailhead is **0.2** mile farther.

Description

Our hike starts out across a tributary creek and descends to a forested flat near the river where The Nature Conservancy houses a manager. Please sign in here, and pick up a pamphlet that introduces you to the area's ecology and to Wintu Indian lore via a short interpretive path.

From the manager's flat our trail heads into a botanical wonderland, wandering down-canyon under the shade of Douglas-fir, dogwood, vine and bigleaf maples, and black and canyon oaks. Frequent forest openings with western azalea, deer brush, elderberry and chokecherry let us marvel at the canyon that surrounds us, an impressive if small wilderness that supports wolverines, mountain lions, spotted owls, bald eagles and other animals no longer common. Never far away, the river alternately riffles and pools, tempting hikers to swim and fishermen to wet a line.

The McCloud River is renowned among fly fishermen as one of the hottest spots in California for wily native rainbow and introduced brown trout. In addition, it has been the southernmost refuge of the Dolly Varden char, a generally northern salmonid that survives only in chilly waters. Though the Ice Ages ended (at least temporarily), the Dolly Varden stayed on in the McCloud because this river derives mostly from cold, profuse springs of Mt. Shasta snowmelt. Unfortunately, the reservoir above the Preserve has gradually damaged the char's habitat by warming the water and diverting much of the flow, and tragically The Nature Conservancy suspects that the McCloud's Dolly Varden has recently become extinct.

Nearly a mile from the trailhead we come to a fork in the trail, where a shortcut climbs gradually over a knoll to rejoin the riverside trail about 1/4 mile down. As we tour down-canyon, we pass through occasional rocky openings of greenschist and limestone. Here we especially need to take care to stay clear of poison oak near the trail. Our trail gradually curves with the river, north then south, crossing Bald Mountain Creek on the way. A bit farther it emerges from forest near Boundary Creek, and the "Big Bend" in the McCloud. About 1/3 mile beyond we come to trail's end; below here The Nature Conservancy reserves the river and the canyon for nature alone, plus occasional scientific study.

The Nature Conservancy depends on private donations to manage its preserves. If you would like to donate money or to volunteer, contact it at:

The McCloud River Preserve
P.O. Box 409
McCloud, CA 96057
(916) 926-4366

The Nature Conservancy
785 Market Street, 3rd Floor
San Francisco, CA 94103
(415) 777-0487

McCloud River Trail

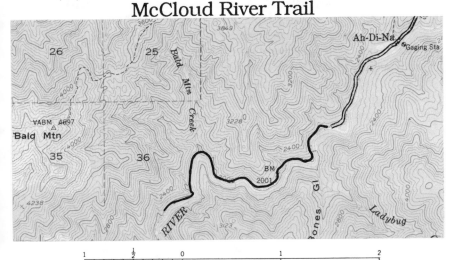

Castle Crags Day Hike
5.6 miles round trip

The Castle Crags startle most drivers on Interstate 5; the granite parapets, spires, pinnacles and domes rise above the surrounding hills with a surreal grandeur. The popular hike described here brings one to some spectacular views right among the crags. While the hike is quite an inspiring climb, it's but an introduction to "The Crags." Acres and acres of towers and hidden valleys extend behind what one can see. Some of the crags are known to climbers, and some of the valleys were hideouts for Indians, but probably some spots have never been visited. A campground and the first half of the trail are in a state park, while most of Castle Crags is national forest wilderness. At present (1990) no permit is needed to enter Castle Crags Wilderness.

Trailhead

From I-5 take the Castella exit, which is 14 miles south of Mount Shasta and 47 miles north of Redding. On the west side of the freeway, keep right and drive past the Castella tavern and post office, and keep right again to reach the entrance to Castle Crags State Park. Here there is a day-use charge, which also admits one to the showers in the campground. From the entrance station follow trailhead signs through the campground onto a steeply switchbacking road, which ends at a trailhead parking lot 1.3 miles from the entrance station.

Description

From the road's last curve our hike leads west on a broad, flat path in the shade of Douglas-firs and black oaks. In 0.3 mile we come to a junction from which a spur trail contours north for 0.6 mile to Root Creek. Our trail continues west and starts climbing, soon arriving at a junction with the Pacific Crest Trail at a clearing for powerlines atop Kettlebelly Ridge. We continue climbing west, back into the forest.

After a couple of steep switchbacks the path rises gradually, turning north around a ridge and climbing past our first close-up view of the crags. To the southwest another group of cliffs, Gray Rocks, pokes up as well. We next arrive at a forested saddle from where a spur trail contours off west for 0.3 mile to Indian Springs, a refreshing oasis shaded by bigleaf maples.

From this junction our trail continues north to a dramatic vista to the 1200-foot east face of Castle Dome, looming over the Root Creek

Castle Dome and Mt. Shasta

drainage, and Mt. Shasta beyond. From here we turn back into the woods for another 1/4 mile before coming upon outlying spires. The trail switchbacks and weaves over a craggy notch, then continues to climb steadily beneath a series of 100-300-foot walls. A long, rising traverse brings us to a few rocky switchbacks and, climbing these brings us to the shoulder below the south face of Castle Dome.

West of this manzanita-covered shoulder some of the other spectacular crags rise in all their bold jaggedness. The Castle Crags are an uplift of granodiorite fairly similar to that of the Sierra, but for reasons unknown lying some distance from that range. Geologists speculate that the Crags—and the entire Klamath region—originally were connected to the present north end of the Sierra, but if so were long ago displaced to the west by some as yet undiscovered faulting.

The maintained trail ends at this shoulder below Castle Dome. However, a use trail winds farther north-northwest through the manzanita, becoming a deeply eroded rut where one must clamber over exposed roots. This rut brings you to the saddle west of Castle Dome, where you can wander among some outcrops and look over the headwaters of Root Creek, an extensive palace of slabs and spires. Take care in scrambling over any rocks, for in places the potential fall

Castle Crags Trail

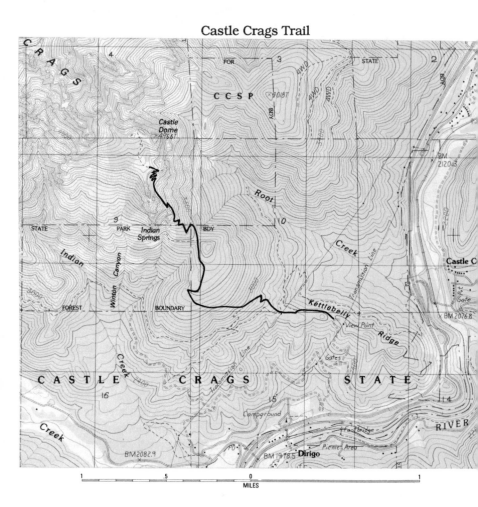

is very serious. A fenced overlook right at the base of Castle Rock offers a particularly breathtaking view.

Castle Lake-Mt. Bradley

10.8 miles round trip

Surprisingly uncrowded, this route climbs from a large subalpine lake, past another smaller lake, to a spectacularly scenic ridge walk.

Trailhead

From downtown Mount Shasta drive southwest across I-5 (on the overpass of the main Mount Shasta exit) to a T at Old Stage Road. Turn left (SW) and after 0.3 mile veer right, toward Lake Siskiyou. Continue across the dam at Lake Siskiyou, and after just a few hundred yards turn left onto Castle Lake Road. This road climbs 7.1 miles to Castle Lake.

Although swimmers, fishermen and sunbathers flock to Castle Lake on summer weekends, the enclosing granite cliffs and forests still reflect in the lake's clear waters, a High Sierra-like setting. Scientists have studied the lake intensely, finding among other things that the lake supports many fish partly because a couple of lakeside alder groves add nitrogen to the waters.

Description

From the very end of the parking lot, walk east across the lake's outlet and pick up our signed trail as it leads south near the lake's east shore. The path promptly starts climbing among open groves of Shasta red-fir and western white pine here, letting us look down on Castle Lake's shimmering surface. We keep left at an unmarked spur, and continue climbing steeply southeast. Our climb soon takes us out of the trees to rocky going through a bonanza of seasonal wildflowers. Brodiaea, mountain pride, stonecrop and mariposa lilies grow among the rusty metamorphic outcrops where we top out at the crest of Castle Lake's basin.

From the saddle here our trail turns east past a small ephemeral pond and starts a steep descent through a dense fir stand. The descent brings us into a verdant meadow, and across this glade under a bluff lies Little Castle Lake. We continue east past the short spur to this lake and hike across the outlet stream. A rollercoaster section of trail then takes us across broken slopes into a fairly level, dense forest. The trail is a bit hard to follow here, but tree blazes mark the way.

Castle Lake and Mt. Shasta

Tree-watchers might notice among the firs a specimen of "weeping," or Brewer, spruce, a fairly rare tree found only in the Klamath-Trinity region.

In this forest the trail abruptly turns south almost straight upslope, and then emerges onto the ridgetop above with a stunning view of the Castle Crags. Few people venture into the northern crags you see from here, and though the view is extensive it includes only about ¹/₅ of the Crag's total extent.

On the trail, once a ridgetop firebreak, we head northeast, and before long the view opens entirely to include Mt. Shasta, Lassen Peak, Mt. Eddy (across Strawberry Valley from Shasta) and Lake Siskiyou. One can continue along the ridgetop, rising and descending in and out of occasional Jeffrey pine groves, to join a road that continues for 0.6 mile to an old Forest Service lookout at Mt. Bradley, 3.4 miles from where we first gained the ridge.

Castle Lake-Mt. Bradley Trail

When hiking back along the ridgetop, keep alert for our trail descending northwest off the ridge back into the woods, because an extension of the ridgeline path continues southwest and disappears into the brush at the head of the drainage to the south.

Black Butte

5.2 miles round trip

Although from nearby Interstate 5 a climb up Black Butte appears to demand a horrific scree struggle, the fact is that a groomed, occasionally rocky trail climbs 2000 feet to its summit, steadily bringing one to some of the most impressive perspectives of Shasta and the region.

Trailhead

Drive 2.0 miles up Everitt Highway, to where the highway starts a long curve right, and turn left (W) onto a dirt road signed for Black Butte. After **0.1** mile turn right (N), and continue for **1.0** mile to a junction. Turn left (W) for **0.4** and then curve right (N), staying on the main dirt road. This soon curves left (W) and after **1.2** miles you reach a junction where you turn left (S). This final leg curves right (W) and climbs very steeply to the trailhead, 5.3 miles from the start of the highway.

Description

Our trail begins with a long, rising arc around Black Butte's north slopes, taking us across talus slopes scattered with white firs, ponderosa pines, Douglas-firs and squaw currant. Brilliantly colored lichens crust over many of the sharp gray blocks of dacite here. As we curve to the north and northwest sides of Black Butte, the hillocks of Shasta Valley come into view, and one can try to imagine the immensity of the landslide off of Shasta that created that bumpy terrain (see the "Geology" Chapter). Beyond rises the symmetrical cone of Mt. McLoughlin, in Oregon.

As we work around to the west slopes of the butte, we see Mt. Eddy rising above I-5 and Strawberry Valley below, and to the southeast we see some of the Castle Crags as well as distant Lassen Peak. Now we cut back northeast through a secluded ravine, a gap between two of Black Butte's four overlapping cones. Along here the trail is at its rockiest, but better tread soon takes us from a red-fir grove to a "near-enough-to-touch" panorama of Mt. Shasta. Always in full view of Shasta now, we continue climbing around to Black Butte's east slopes, then cut back to the north, not far from the summit. Tighter switchbacks occupy our last 1/4 mile to the top, where all the panoramas we've seen come together in a breathtaking 360° view of the region.

Black Butte Trail

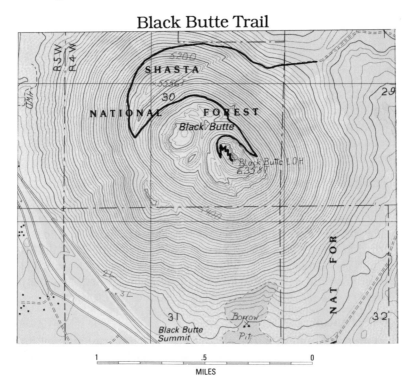

Sisson-Callahan Trail
12.2 miles

Running from subalpine lakes and meadows to lowland Transition forest and chaparral, this historical trail is an introduction to the botanically rich Trinity Mountains. It also offers a side trip to the top of Mt. Eddy, where perhaps the most overwhelming view of Mt. Shasta awaits.

As a route the Sisson-Callahan dates back, if not to Indians, then to trappers, prospectors and cattlemen of the mid-1800s. As a Forest Service trail it dates to 1911, when its construction linked Forest Headquarters in Sisson (Mount Shasta) with Callahan. The west half of the trail, beyond Parks Creek Summit, is traceable, but it is largely masked by logging and mining roads. However, the east half, described here, passes through nearly uninterrupted backcountry, and has been designated a National Recreation Trail.

As described here, the hike leads from Parks Creek Summit on the Pacific Crest Trail, and then takes the Sisson-Callahan route over Deadfall Summit and down the north fork of the Sacramento River to another trailhead near Lake Siskiyou. To hike its entirety one needs either to arrange a car shuttle or to plan a long round trip—too long for most hikers in one day. Many hikers, however, make a day of walking into Deadfall lakes and back. For the full hike, most people prefer to start at higher Parks Creek Summit for a net descent of 3200 feet to the Lake Siskiyou trailhead.

Trailheads

To reach Parks Creek Summit, drive north on I-5 3.4 miles past the Weed turnoff and take the Edgewood-Gazelle exit. Turn southwest under the freeway under the freeway to a T, and turn right (NW). After 0.4 mile turn left (SW) onto unsigned Stewart Springs Road—Forest Road 17. After driving 3.9 miles up this road, keep right and continue as the road steepens, staying on paved Road 17 to the summit, 12.9 miles from the Stewart Springs turnoff.

To get to the eastern trailhead, from downtown Mount Shasta cross I-5 at the main Mount Shasta exit and continue southwest to a T at Old Stage Road. Turn left (S) and soon veer right onto W.A. Barr Road, toward Lake Siskiyou. A mile from the Old Stage turnoff, turn right onto North Shore Road 40N27. Drive along the north shore of Lake Siskiyou, keeping left at the only minor fork, and park near

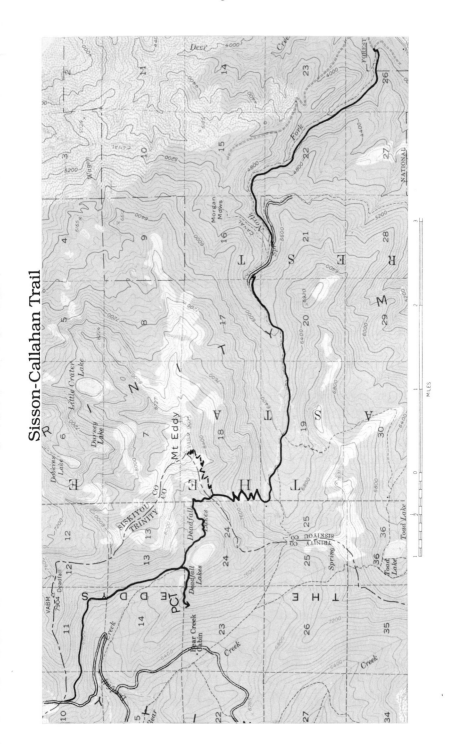

Sisson-Callahan Trail

where the road ends at the North Fork of the Sacramento River. Here the hike starts on an old roadbed that heads up the opposite side of the river.

Description

From Parks Creek Summit we strike southeast on the well-groomed Pacific Crest Trail, sampling a diverse forest unique to the Trinity Mountains. We pass beneath red firs, white firs, Douglas-firs, western white pines and lodgepole pines as we generally contour in a long arc to Deadfall Creek. When we reach the creek we intersect the Sisson-Callahan Trail proper. From here the PCT continues south to round a ridge into Bear Creek drainage. To the northwest the Sisson-Callahan Trail heads down Deadfall Creek and becomes an old 4WD track that meets the paved road. We take the Sisson-Callahan Trail southeast, up Deadfall Creek's drainage.

Now we enjoy meadows, forest and high views ahead to Mt. Eddy on our steady climb, which before long steepens up a shallow ravine. Out of sight just to the south and west lie the lowermost Deadfall lakes, the largest of which offers a particularly refreshing swim. Then we reach a bench containing one of the Deadfall lakes, and we circle along its west shore, eyeing the waters for the trout that make this basin a favorite with fishermen. Next we hop a stream and rise to a slightly higher bench that cups one of the larger of the lakes, a subalpine gem reflecting the craggy ochre face of Mt. Eddy. After cruising along the meadowy south shore of this lake, we start the final climb to Deadfall Summit.

A single switchback takes us south out of the last lake's small cirque and up through one of the most diverse stands of conifers you'll ever see; on these slopes grow red fir, white fir, lodgepole pine, western white pine, whitebark pine and foxtail pine. It's thought that during recent eras these Trinity mountains have been a refuge for many different plant species. Alternating glaciations and droughts elsewhere have created stresses for many species, and as a moist semicoastal range holding only small glaciers, the Klamath-Trinitys have maintained a steadier climate for plants driven from the south during droughts, and others pushed from the north during snowy periods.

The short final climb to Deadfall Summit gives us a distant view west beyond the Deadfall basin over the subalpine ridge country of Scott Mountain and over much of the rest of the Trinity River's headwaters. We cross the pass into the Sacramento River watershed, and about 100 yards east of the crest we come to a cairn, which marks the spot where those who want to climb Mt. Eddy will branch north (see inset).

Mt. Eddy Ascent
2.8 miles round trip, 1000-foot gain

Although no trail to Mt. Eddy is obvious from the Sisson-Callahan Trail, it's not hard to leave the latter track and find the old trail built to service the now-abandoned lookout atop Mt. Eddy. About 100 yards southeast of Deadfall Summit, head east-northeast on a gradually ascending traverse. In about 0.1 mile you should pick up the trail near the first switchback. If not, head more directly upslope, and you'll soon come across a very clear track.

The first few switchbacks climb through a surprisingly dense stand of foxtail pine, an uncommon relative of the bristlecone pine which grows only in these mountains and in the southern Sierra. The switchbacks touch the Trinity-Sacramento divide a couple of times, and then one long switchback cuts back east onto slopes where scattered whitebark pines gradually replace the foxtails. Now a steady bank of tighter switchbacks climbs into the rocky alpine realm of hulsea, penstemon and *krummholz* whitebarks.

The toil to the summit rewards one with a stunning view of Mt. Shasta. Perhaps from no other place can one feel so intensely the overwhelming immensity of Shasta. Atop Mt. Eddy a vestigial lookout still stands, though it was abandoned in 1931.

Continuing on the Sisson-Callahan Trail, we start a steep descent south off the pass, braking through duff down into a meadowy realm of fir and chinquapin. Before too long switchbacks ease the grade, and on the easternmost of these hairpins we come within 100 yards of a gushing spring, which, along with springs on Mt. Shasta, is one of the sources of the Sacramento River. Depression-era license plates high on the trees mark our trail as an old snow-survey route, and eventually we pass near the surveyor's old cabin.

Turning southeast here, we continue on a more gradually descending traverse past a junction with a faint trail that runs west back over the divide. Our trail becomes a bit obscure also, but numerous tree blazes guide us on a continued downhill traverse to the North Fork of the Sacramento, at this point a quiet stream that we hop across on stones. Here another old trail heads southwest to Toad Lake, but we continue east down the Sacramento, ambling through glades and groves of white fir, lodgepole pine and surprisingly large incense-cedars. As we reach gentler, soggier ground the glades become richer with brodiaea, potentilla, columbine and yarrow, allowing broader views to ridgelines composed of russet-yellow peridotite that rim the valley.

At one meadow the grasses have partly overgrown the trail, and we continue on a straight course across the north side of this meadow to find a dry, rocky creekbed that after a short distance leads into distinct trail. Paralleling the North Fork of the Sacramento, our gentle descent continues for another half mile, to where a couple of switchbacks start our drop out of the once-glaciated high country into the river's lower canyon. The switchbacks empty us onto an old roadbed, which we follow for nearly 0.5 mile before coming to a SISSON-CALLAHAN trail marker on the north edge of the road. At this post, unfortunately easy to miss without a watchful eye, we drop off the road and start a steady descent along the now-tumbling Sacramento River.

Under sugar pines, Jeffrey pines and Douglas-firs our trail follows the river canyon's curve to the southeast, passing an old jeep road that climbs south, and then descending on a couple of small switchbacks. We continue descending past a waterfall and into warmer climes, where beargrass, pipsissiwa, paintbrush, Shasta lily and azalea catch our eye. As we descend farther, breaks in the forest let us look back for a last glimpse at the eastern summits of Mt. Eddy. Eventually our trail runs onto an old roadbed, which takes us across a tributary creek and curves east down to the old crossing of the main river. Here we can hop rocks or perhaps wet our feet to ford to the eastern trailhead, on North Shore Road.

Deadfall Lakes basin from Deadfall Summit

Pluto Cave

Many volcanic regions have what are called lava tubes, caves formed when the outer surface of a lava flow cools and congeals, but the still-molten core flows on and evacuates the congealed shell. A number of lava tubes are found around Shasta, some of which are a mile or more long, and the most famous is Pluto Cave.

Venturing into this large cave should not be taken lightly. The depths of Pluto Cave are eternally dark, so take at least two working flashlights; headlamps are better, to keep your hands free. The temperature inside remains a cool 50°, so bring warm clothes. The way is occasionally quite rocky, so wear sturdy footgear and choose your steps carefully. Finally, don't go alone. While the seriousness of somehow getting lost in the cave should not be overlooked, for those who are careful the eerie experience of advancing into a seemingly infinite blackness is unforgettable.

Trailhead

From the Weed stoplight, drive northeast on Highway 97 for 10.6 miles to County Road A12. On it go northwest 3.3 miles, and at the end of a long, gentle downgrade turn left (W) onto a dirt road. In 1988 a powerline pole at this turnoff had the words PLUTO CAVE inscribed vertically. Drive west and southwest on this road for about 0.3 mile, to where it's no longer passable.

Description

Here, at a large juniper tree, the track forks, and either fork will take you to the cave. If you walk west-southwest on the right-hand

Pluto Cave

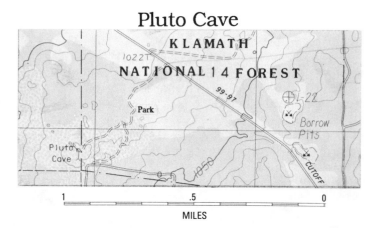

MILES

In Pluto Cave

fork for about ¼ mile, you follow spray-painted rocks and come to a large depression in the ground; this is the vague beginning of Pluto Cave. Walk right (N) a short distance along the rim of the depression to a path descending into it.

If you walk southwest on the left-hand fork, after about ¼ mile you come onto a well-graded cinder road. Walk west down this for a short distance to a mound of blocks. Among these blocks is the more distant entrance to the cave. Walk north into the entrance and soon you'll come to an opening, the depression mentioned in the other road fork. A path runs northwest through the surprisingly lush floor of the depression, leading you to the depths of Pluto Cave.

The dusty path leads between boulders into growing darkness. But this is only a preliminary darkness, for you soon come underneath some large gaps in the 20 foot-high ceiling of the cave. Some graffiti on the walls date to the turn of the century, and it's interesting to contrast the careful hand of the earlier adventurers with today's spray-painted scrawls. After about ⅛ mile you pass the last light, and descend into absolute darkness. A rocky, dusty track leads on, with occasional spots where you have to scramble across boulders. The way continues farther than most are inclined to venture—at least a mile.

Castle Crags

Steeped in history and legend, the rugged granite of Castle Crags is a jagged contrast to symmetrical volcanic Mt. Shasta just across the valley. During the early 1850s a brief but unsuccessful gold rush strained both the environment and relations with the Indians living near the Crags. Joaquin Miller, later known as "the poet of the Sierra," lived for a time in the area chronicling the history, and helped to perpetrate legends of lost Indian gold. In 1855 a battle was fought with the Indians in which Miller claimed to have been wounded. It was likely the last time in the West in which Indians relied exclusively upon bows and arrows. Battle Mountain, an impressive 1500-foot wall on the west side of the Crags, was named for this battle.

For many years pioneers and settlers travelled through the area on the old California-Oregon trail. In 1886 the Southern Pacific Railroad was put through the Sacramento River canyon, effectively opening the country to mining and lumbering. Resorts prospered near the Crags' many mineral springs, and Castle Rock Mineral Water became famous throughout California. Diligent efforts by a far-sighted local citizenry resulted in the acquisition of the Crags in 1933 by the newly formed California State Parks System. In 1984, 7300 acres adjacent to the Park were designated as a federal wilderness area.

Castle Crags State Park has 64 drive-in family campsites and a special walk-in area for backpackers and Pacific Crest Trail hikers, Picnicking, hiking, fishing and swimming are the most popular activities; you can enjoy several miles of improved trails within the Park, including 2 miles of riverside trail. The Pacific Crest Trail runs through the Park yielding magnificent views of the Crags from varying perspectives, and some outstanding glimpses of nearby Mt. Shasta. The Crags are also a relatively unused venue for rock climbing. You can obtain climbing information at Park Headquarters or at The Fifth Season outdoor shop in Mount Shasta. For further information:

Castle Crags State Park
P.O. Box 80
Castella, CA 96017-0080
(916) 235-2684

Castle Crags from the air

4　Climbing

The high mountains have a special allure for those who go up into the cirques and high meadows, and onto the aretes and peaks. Life itself seems more sparkling as the mountains become our window to a richer, clearer reality. The variety of our mountain experiences can be endless: There are different paths to be followed in climbing mountains—different personal "paths" as well as different routes on the peaks.

Although a great mountain like Shasta has special rewards for those who venture onto it, life on the heights is not always easy, and our goals may be hard to achieve. Certainly even the best mountaineers and other outdoorsmen have known discomfort, difficulty and even fear. In fact, knowledge and understanding of adversity are what set the seasoned adventurer apart from those with less experience.

The enjoyment, challenge and satisfaction of climbing should always be tempered with concern for safety. This book can help you discover some wonderful, exciting places on Mt. Shasta, but it's no substitute for experience, careful preparations and good judgement. You are responsible for your own safety. To ensure it, you must get proper mountaineering training and then exercise caution and common sense based on that training plus experience. Many outdoor organizations and clubs, and college and university recreation programs, have mountaineering courses. These courses are a good way to learn climbing from experienced climbers.

Mt. Shasta shows many changes and many moods over the seasons. A climb up the John Muir/Avalanche Gulch route during the long, calm days of early summer is usually sublime. The same climb during winter can be very serious and difficult. During ample snow years many of the northside and eastside routes remain in excellent condition with hard snow throughout the summer and fall. However, in drier years, and generally by autumn of normal years, they can become glassy ice. We recommend that you always check weather and snow conditions before starting a hike or a climb. We also urge you to be honest with yourself and your climbing partners regarding your goals, experience, gear requirements, and even your mind-set. Mountains must be met on their own terms. Therefore, take responsibility for your judgment, actions and welfare.

Many emergencies have taken place on Mt. Shasta, and rescue is often lengthy, dangerous and uncertain. Rescues may be delayed by unfavorable weather, unavailability of helicopters able to fly in the thin air of the upper altitudes, hazards to rescuers and other things.

The Siskiyou County Sheriff's Department is responsible for coordinating rescue efforts on Mt. Shasta. They offer a (voluntary) register for climbers at the Mount Shasta Ranger District offices (204 E. Alma St., Mount Shasta; (916) 926-4511), and at their local substation (111-A E. Lake St., Mount Shasta; (916) 926-2552 or 911), but unless an accident is known to have occurred, they will not take action until *after* your expected return date has passed.

We've chosen what we think are the finest routes on Mt. Shasta, along with some selected variations. The route descriptions are fairly general—partly because the mountain is never quite the same from season to season, and partly so as not to deprive you of a sense of adventure. Many of the routes do not require a rope, but most require ice ax and crampons, and knowledge of their use. Other routes require more experience, specialized equipment, glacier training and crevasse rescue knowledge. Some of the summit routes are quite long if started from base camp, so we've mentioned some high camps to break the climb into shorter days, if you choose. The climbing routes are listed clockwise around the mountain beginning on the southwest side at the historic John Muir/Avalanche Gulch climb.

Ratings of difficulty are highly subjective, and will vary due to weather and climbing conditions, strength of party, and other factors. We've drawn from the American rating system—which takes into consideration difficulty, continuity, time, exposure and commitment to give a numerical "class" rating—and simplified the ratings as follows:

D1: 3rd class. Moderate terrain and moderate conditions, either rock or snow, requiring proper footwear, ice ax and crampons. A rope is generally not needed, but may be taken in reserve for less experienced members.

Example: D1   R 1, John Muir/Avalanche Gulch
R 3, Sargents Ridge

D2:   4th class. A rope is necessary for belaying and protection but the climbing is not very difficult. Traveling on crevassed glaciers may be necessary, but the terrain and route finding are moderate.

Examples: R 5   Casaval Ridge
             R 8   Bolam Glacier

D3   Similar to 5th class. Difficult ice and snow or rock requiring specialized equipment and advanced technique. The glaciers may have steep icefalls, many crevasses and difficult route finding.

Example: R 11   Hotlum Glacier

Times listed are conservative averages for round trip from base camp. Actual time can vary greatly due to weather, snow and ice conditions, strength of party and other reasons. Times are indicated in days and fractions thereof.

Access to the trailheads is described in detail in the "Hiking" Chapter. The best base camp and high-camp locations are indicated.

AREA: Southwest Side of Mt. Shasta From Sargents Ridge to Cascade Gulch

Route 1:	**Traditional John Muir/Avalanche Gulch**
Difficulty:	1
Access:	Everitt Memorial Highway via Bunny or Sand Flat
Campsites:	Horse Camp, Helen Lake, Sand Flat, Bunny Flat
Time:	1 day

Description

This was the route of the first recorded ascent of Mt. Shasta, by Captain E.D. Pearce in 1854, and is by far the most popular climbing route today. In the early days, before improved roads and all-weather highways, a climb began on horseback in Strawberry Valley in the

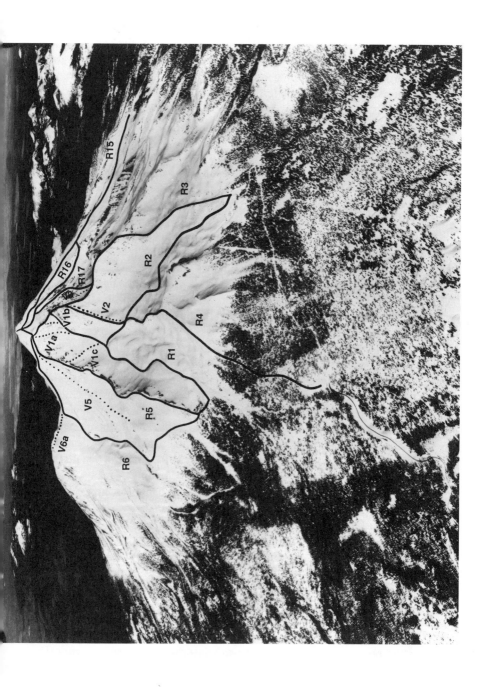

town of Sisson. In those days guides and outfitters led their parties to timberline near the site of the present-day Sierra Club cabin at Horse Camp. Here, meadows provided forage and water for the horses while the party climbed. Over the years increased use of this area brought improvement of the trail, construction of Olberman's Causeway, and establishment of campsites. Nevertheless, Horse Camp is still remarkably much like it was a century ago. There is still the gathering and the camaraderie of climbers from the world over, a summer custodian is in residence at the cabin to help the first-time visitor, and the evenings are still the catalysts of tall tales. From the stone benches lining the rear wall of the cabin, you can see the panorama and many features of this climbing route. This is a wonderful base camp for one's first climb on Mt. Shasta.

From the Sierra Club cabin to the summit is only 4.1 miles, but over 6000 vertical feet! From a viewpoint just behind the cabin, the foreground vista (and the beginning of the climb) can be divided into three areas, from left to right: The climber's gully, the middle moraines and Avalanche Gulch. Olberman's Causeway, laboriously built of huge, flat stones by the cabin's first custodian, Mac Olberman, begins just a few feet behind the cabin and heads you in the proper direction. We follow the causeway as it leads toward the peak. (When the causeway is still covered with snow, ascend the broad, main drainage behind the cabin.) Continue up the long climber's gully, which curves left, then straightens and opens up to a broad area of gentle flats and rock moraine. You are now at the left (W) of the huge, open drainage called Avalanche Gulch. Ascend moderate slopes upward to a flat area at 10,400 feet known as Helen Lake. You can also reach Helen Lake by ascending the morainal hills, or steps, just right (E) of the climber's gully. This line is a little more direct, but also steeper in places. Conditions at the time will dictate the best choice; consolidated snow is always easier climbing than loose talus. Few climbers use Avalanche Gulch proper as a means of ascent to Helen Lake, but it's often an excellent ski descent route.

Helen Lake was named in 1924 when Helen Wheeler, guided on a successful summit climb by Ed Stuhl, inquired as to the name of the lovely tarn. Ed christened the tiny lake on the spot, and the name has stuck ever since. Actually, the lake is usually under snow, and hence seldom seen except late in exceptionally dry years. During the drought years of 1975-77, and again in 1988, Helen Lake was visible and worthy of its name. If you wish to establish a higher base camp than Horse Camp, the bench at Helen Lake makes an excellent, and often popular, campsite. Except in winter and early spring, runoff

Climbers on traditional route above Avalanche Gulch

water is usually available, and a number of flat, protected campsites have evolved over the years. Increased use of this fragile alpine environment necessitated the installation of a pit toilet by the U.S. Forest Service in 1988 at the east of Helen Lake. (In winter, locate your latrine *away* from the lake area.)

Above Helen Lake lies the most strenuous section of the route, a 2500-foot snowfield that steepens to 35° near its top. Stay right of center of the main drainage, aiming generally toward the right side of the Red Banks, the prominent orange palisades of welded pumice which represent one of Shasta's more recent flows. Constant vigilance is advised; the Red Banks are the source of most of the rockfall in Avalanche Gulch. Allow yourself plenty of time to climb and return before the sun's heat can loosen and dislodge any rocks. Mid to late summer is the most dangerous time, although rockfall can occur during *any* season and at *any* time. At nearly 12,000 feet, stay to the right of a large rockfield called the Heart. Depending on the time of year and the previous year's snowpack, this feature may take on a variety of sizes and shapes. The Heart can also be a source of rockfall.

The little saddle between the Red Banks and Thumb Rock at 12,800 feet is a good place to rest, eat and warm up in the sun; a small alcove can provide protection in case of wind. Now walk briefly around behind the Red Banks on the edge of the Konwakiton Glacier, avoid-

Climbing through one of the Red Banks chimneys

ing the crevasse (called a bergschrund) where the glacier snow has pulled away from the rock. Regain the Red Banks and follow the ridge to its top, a broad snowfield bounded on the north by the Whitney Glacier and on the south by the Konwakiton Glacier. In mid-to-late summer the bergschrund can be quite large, blocking easy return to the Red Banks' crest. Snowbridges across this bergschrund may offer safe passage in the cool of the morning, but they can be dangerously softened by the afternoon sun. If so, or if your lack of equipment and experience or your intuition causes doubt, you can backtrack a few hundred feet and climb upward through one of several shallow gullies in the Red Banks, reaching their top shortly.

A short but worthwhile side trip is a brief walk north on the snowfield at the top of the Red Banks. Here, you can enjoy a view of the whole expanse of the Whitney Glacier, the longest glacier in California. In mid-season, Clarence King Lake (within Shastina's crater) and Sisson Lake (on the saddle between Shasta and Shastina) appear as turquoise jewels against the stark white backdrop of snow. Continue up "Misery Hill" (either a misnomer or an understatement, depending upon conditions) via the best-quality snow or a faint scree trail right of center of the hill. You soon reach the flat summit snowfield. Cross this plateau, heading for an obvious col between the summit pinnacle to the right (E), and a smaller one to the west. The summit snowfield is often wind-sculpted into a labyrinth of bizarre and beautiful shapes. During late season, and in years of light snowpack, the twisted cylindrical remains of the old geodetic monument may be seen emerging from snow beneath the southwest face of the summit pinnacle. The bubbling sulfur fumaroles nearby are a reminder that Mt. Shasta is indeed a volcano, active not long ago.

Ascend the summit via easy scrambling on its northwest side, thus concluding Mt. Shasta's most historic and most popular route.

Descend via the same route.

Variation 1a: Left of Heart
Difficulty: 2
Time: 1 + days

Description

During unusually dry seasons, and late in the summer, this drainage usually holds snow longer than the traditional route to the right, offering better climbing for those who are experienced on steep slopes. Climb increasingly steep snow fields above Helen Lake until you're beneath the imposing north end of Red Banks. Depending upon seasonal conditions, several icy chimneys offer challenging passages through the palisades. The chimneys become shorter and easier the farther left (N) you go along the Red Banks, although steep snow cornices often overhang at the extreme left end. If so, a short ridge left (N) of the Red Bank abuts the very top of Casaval Ridge, and offers passage around the cornices. You are now atop the Red Banks and at the base of Misery Hill, slightly north of the traditional route, which may be followed to the summit.

Descend the same route, or Route 1.

Variation 1b   Red Banks Chimneys

Difficulty: 2
Time: 1 day

Description

During times when the Konwakiton Glacier bergschrund presents difficulties (see Route 1 description), these variations are enjoyable, time-saving detours. When climbing the traditional route (Route 1), you pass beneath the Red Banks for several hundred feet before reaching a saddle at Thumb Rock. At the lowest point of the Red Banks is a huge, cleft rock outcropping that looks like a caricature valentine. Just right of this "heart" (not the same as the rock island below of that name) is a deep, snow-filled chimney leading all the way to the top of the Red Banks. A few hundred feet right of this chimney is another landmark—a mushroom- or anvil-shaped rock. This rock may also be passed on either side to reach the top of the Red Banks.

Descend via Route 1, although the chimneys may be descended if they are not too icy.

Variation 1c   Upper Casaval Ridge

Difficulty: 2 to 3
Time: 1+ days

Description

Looking north from Helen Lake, you can see a broad shoulder descending from Casaval Ridge. This shoulder is much less steep than any other rib or gully descending from Casaval Ridge. This is the "second window," a common escape, or bail-out, from Route 5. This route variation is an excellent portal for gaining access to the upper reaches of Casaval Ridge late in the season when the lower parts of the ridge lack snow. Follow Casaval ridge to its top, then the traditional route (Route 1) to the summit.

Descend either your ascent route or Route 1, depending on conditions and time.

Route 2:   Old Ski Bowl

Difficulty:	1
Access:	Everitt Memorial Highway, Panther Meadows
Campsites:	Panther Meadow, old Ski Bowl lodge parking area
Time:	1 day

Description

The original Ski Bowl was opened in 1959, and it remained in operation until 1978 when weather, financial problems, and a lift-destroying avalanche forced its closure. All that remain are the lodge and the parking lot. Until the Ski Bowl closed, Everitt Memorial Highway was regularly plowed its full 14-mile length. This enabled year-round access to Sargents Ridge and many excellent cross-country and ski-mountaineering routes. Now the road is plowed only as far as Bunny Flat, and the remaining 3 miles to Panther Meadows and the Ski Bowl are left to thaw on their own, usually by the end of June.

From the Ski Bowl parking lot, a maze of old dirt service roads winds upward through a cirque to the location of the old top terminal at 9200 feet where several radiotelephone antennas remain. From this location, head directly north until intersecting Green Butte Ridge, the southern margin of vast Avalanche Gulch. Follow the ridge to a gap just north of Point 9572, then contour left to the traditional route (Route 1) near Helen Lake. Since the last 3 miles of Everitt Memorial Highway are no longer plowed, access to this route is seldom open until late June or early July. By then, there are long stretches of scree and talus on the climbing route.

Descend your route of ascent.

Variation 2	Green Butte Ridge to Sargents Ridge(R 3)
Difficulty:	2
Time:	1+ days

Description

Instead of traversing left to the traditional John Muir route, continue climbing Green Butte Ridge until it joins Sargents Ridge at 12,000 feet. Follow Sargents Ridge (R 3) to its juncture with the traditional route (R 1) at Thumb Rock.

Descend via the climbing route.

Route 3:	Sargents Ridge
Difficulty:	2
Access:	Everitt Memorial Highway
Campsites	Same as Route 2
Time:	1+ days

Description

Named for John Sargent, a forest ranger who enjoyed climbing Mt. Shasta in the 1940s, this ridge is an excellent winter route because of its general lack of avalanche exposure. Summer popularity has waned in recent years because late openings of the last three miles of Everitt Memorial Highway have prevented easy access. By mid to late summer, lack of snow on the route makes for some unpleasant climbing over talus and scree. It's worth the effort, however, in winter and spring, to ski or snowshoe from Bunny Flat to a base camp in the old Ski Bowl to climb this route.

From any of many good campsites in the Ski Bowl cirque, climb northeast on gentle shoulders that join the ridge proper. A good landmark is Shastarama Point (Point 11,135). Beyond this large outcropping, the ridge flattens for a quarter mile. Here you'll have excellent views of the Mud Creek and the Konwakiton glaciers, as well as the impressive, precipitous depths of Mud Creek Canyon. Continue upward on the steepening ridge, avoiding obstacles and exposure by bearing left. Join Route 1 at the Red Banks-Thumb Rock saddle and follow it to the summit.

Descend the climbing route, or Route 1 to the Ski Bowl traverse (R 2).

Co-author Zanger glissading in late June

Variation 3   Traverse to Mud Creek Glacier
Difficulty: 2
Time: 1 day

Description

From the long, flat ridge just beyond Shastarama Point, a short traverse to the east takes you to the small Mud Creek Glacier. This glacier has a stark, alpine beauty and is seldom visited. There is also a beautiful hidden lake behind Shastarama Point.

Descend via the approach route.

Route 4:   Green Butte Ridge
Difficulty: 1 to 2
Access: Everitt Memorial Highway
Campsite: Bunny Flat
Time: 1+ days

Description

This route and the old Ski Bowl route (R 2) share a distinction: while nor particularly aesthetic or notable, these routes are popular among climbers with limited time because one can start climbing right from a parking lot and avoid any hike into a base camp. In recent years, however, with road plowing to the Ski Bowl discontinued, Green Butte Ridge has become more popular as an accessible and safe winter route.

From the parking area at Bunny Flat, climb northeast on gentle, forested slopes until you're above timberline and level with Green Butte, the large, rounded shoulder at 9200 feet which juts outward to the south. Continue northeast on Green Butte ridge to join the Sargents Ridge route (R 3), or traverse to the traditional route (R 1) as in the Ski Bowl (R 2) route description.

Descend via the climbing route.

Route 5:   Casaval Ridge
Difficulty: 3
Access: Everitt Memorial Highway
Campsites: Same as R 1
Time: 2 to 2+ days

Description

Casaval Ridge is the striking, cockscomb-like ridge north of Avalanche Gulch. Worldly mountaineers compare this to famous classics of the Alps. The route offers an excellent winter ascent and an airy, stimulating spring and early summer climb. Ample bivvy sites add to the attraction of the climb. After early summer the route is not recommended due to lack of snow and much loose rock.

From the Sierra Club cabin at Horse Camp, a broad toe of the ridge is only a few hundred yards north. Climb this wide ridge to about 9800 feet where it makes a jog to the left and joins serrated Casaval Ridge proper. The first part of the ridge is fairly low-angle; you can go around towers blocking the way on either side, but left (N) is usually easier. The ridge begins to increase in steepness at 10,800 feet, a little

Crevasse rescue practice on the Hotlum Glacier

above Helen Lake, which is visible to the right (S). This part of the ridge, called the "first window," offers escape to Helen Lake via moderate slopes on the right. The route steepens at this point, but there are many wide sections. A second escape, the "second window," occurs at 11,800. Here, another broad, moderate slope curves down into Avalanche Gulch above Helen Lake. (During times of avalanche danger, it's unwise to descend into main Avalanche Gulch.) There are a few short, steep sections on the ridge at 13,000 feet. This route joins Route 1 at 13,500 feet and continues to the summit.

Descend either the climbing route, or one of the Avalanche Gulch routes as time and conditions dictate.

Variation 5	The West Face Gully
Difficulty:	2 to 3
Access:	Everitt Memorial Highway
Campsites:	Same as Route 1
Time:	1 to 2 days

Description
North of Casaval Ridge is a beautiful, long gully that begins in Hidden Valley at 9700 feet and ends nearly 4000 feet later at the broad snowfield at the base of Misery Hill. This rarely done route retains snow long into summer, and is an excellent alternative route when Casaval Ridge is too rocky and devoid of snow to be pleasant or safe.

Begin the climb from a high camp in Hidden Valley. If you begin the climb from the lower stretches of Casaval Ridge, you must traverse north to the gully. When the gully begins to narrow at its top, stay left of the dark orange palisades—the westernmost volcanic flow of the Red Banks.

Descend either the route of ascent or Cascade Gulch and the West Ridge (R 6).

Route 6:	Cascade Gulch
Difficulty:	1
Access:	Everitt Memorial Highway
Campsites:	Bunny Flat, Sand Flat, Horse Camp
Time:	1 to 2 days

Description
The famous geologist Clarence King, who is credited with discovering the glaciers on Mt. Shasta, made one of the first ascents of this route, in 1870. Clarence King Lake, within Shastina's crater, was

named after him. From the Sierra Club cabin at Horse Camp, traverse and gradually climb north. Cross several gullies until you reach Hidden Valley at 9200 feet. A good landmark visible from the cabin is a spire of rock (Point 9487) that coincides closely with true north. This spire is on the ridge above Hidden Valley. The valley floor makes an excellent, well-protected high camp. Stay left of the main watercourse—and the waterfall at the head of Hidden Valley—and climb upward to the 12,000 foot saddle between Shasta and Shastina. Climb east along Shasta's wide west ridge, avoiding some steep drop-offs onto the Whitney Glacier, to a point atop the Red Banks and a little west of Misery Hill. Join Route 1 here and continue to the summit.

Descend the climbing route or Route 1.

Variation 6a   Ascent of Shastina
Difficulty: 1
Time: 1 day

Description

From the Shasta-Shastina saddle a short scramble leads west to Shastina's summit pinnacle. Shastina's crater is over a half mile across and several hundred feet deep. Clarence King Lake looks like a turquoise jewel when it becomes free from the crater's snow in midsummer.

Variation 6b   Upper Whitney Glacier to Summit
Difficulty: 2 to 3
Time: 2 days

Description

The upper Whitney Glacier is very smooth compared to the chaotic middle and lower parts of the glacier, and offers pleasant climbing without many crevasses. From the Shasta-Shastina saddle ascend the west ridge a few hundred feet until the easiest entry to the glacier presents itself. Usually, several snowfields spill over onto the glacier from the ridge, providing convenient access. Avoid descending directly from the saddle to the glacier, as a bergschrund and icy cliffs can be dangerous. If you climb too high on the west ridge, some short rock faces prevent easy entry to the glacier. Climb upward, curving east on the glacier, and follow rock ribs to the summit plateau. Descend either the climbing route or the west ridge (R 6).

Shastina, from northwest slopes of Shasta summit

AREA: Shastina to the Hotlum-Bolam Ridge

From Diller Canyon clockwise around Shastina to the Whitney Glacier are many shallow gullies. The climbing is generally arduous because of large amounts of talus and loose rock. Diller Canyon is often climbed in conjunction with a ski descent, but in times of little snow, loose 4th class rock makes the last 1000 feet undesirable.

Route 7:	**Whitney Glacier**
Difficulty:	2 to 3
Access:	Whitney Falls. An eastern fork of the Bolam road allows higher access for 4WD vehicles.
Campsites:	Whitney, Bolam and unnamed intermittent creeks
Time:	2+ days

Description

The Whitney Glacier was named for Professor Josiah D. Whitney, the leader of a famed survey and scientific exploration of Mt. Shasta in 1862. This is California's largest glacier. The glacier stretches for well over 2 miles, and its foot is covered with an enormous quantity of rubble and debris. A base camp on the lower glacier is an experience for the senses: With the towering flanks of Shastina rising over 4000 feet to the west and the long, broad Whitney-Bolam ridge bordering the cavernous canyon on the east, the tableau looks like the Alaska Range or the Himalaya. In early evening's shadows or by moonlight, the scale and the vastness of the scene seems totally different from their daytime aspect. Add to this the constant creaking and grinding of the glacial ice, the irregular sounds of water, and the cannonades and crescendoes of rockfalls and breaking seracs, all contributing to a dramatic alpine setting.

From either the Whitney Creek or Bolam road access, there are many base camp choices. In winter or early spring, you can approach easily on skis, with several comfortable benches for base camp. In summer, it's usually best to set up base camp on the flat lower glacier. There are also some miniature meadows and springs near timberline just west of the glacier terminus, but these can be difficult to find.

Climbing the lower glacier is relatively straightforward, but there might be minor route-finding problems in late summer and fall as

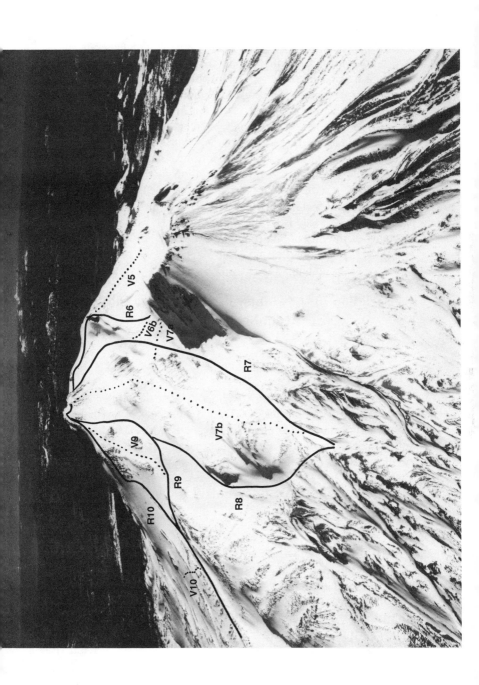

small crevasses begin to open. Avoid venturing close to Shastina's flanks because of the threat of rockfall, and be wary of a similar threat from the upper slopes of Shasta. The center of the lower glacier is generally safest. Depending on the time of year, the enormous icefall adjacent to the Shasta-Shastina saddle is the only major obstacle along the route. In early season several paths may become visible, but the glacial geography is an ever-changing kaleidoscope in three dimensions, and you must be prepared to use your best skills and judgment to improvise a route. In late summer and fall the enormity of the crevasses and the bergschrund spanning full glacier width, and the precariousness of the seracs, give an entirely different and very serious condition to the icefall. By then, literally *acres* of seracs have toppled and avalanched, mostly during the heat of midday. Either side of this icefall section can offer reasonably safe passage. The east side is a little more direct; the west side offers the sanctuary of the Shasta-Shastina saddle, but can be steeper in places. Above the icefall, follow the smooth upper glacier to the summit plateau.

Descend the climbing route.

Variation 7a   Whitney Icefall for Serac and Ice Climbing

Difficulty: 3
Time: 2+ days

Description

When the ice conditions are at their best, the main icefall is a worthy objective for ice-climbing practice. There is sufficient ice most of the time except in midwinter, when the icefall is covered with snow. In summer, warm temperatures can create extremely unstable conditions within the icefall, and seracs can topple at any time.

Variation 7b   Whitney-Bolam Ridge

Difficulty: 1 to 2
Time: 1 to 2 days

Description

This seldom-done variation is very nice when there is sufficient snow-pack; without the snowpack, it's an unenjoyable trudge through loose talus. This ridge can provide a quicker descent to base camp than the Whitney Glacier itself, and it times of adequate snow it is an outstanding ski descent route. The route may be done in its entirety, or you can traverse east from the Whitney Glacier onto the ridge to avoid the Whitney icefall.

Upper Whitney Glacier

From base camp the route appears as a series of gentle shoulders arranged like ascending steps. Follow the path of least resistance over the steps; bearing west is usually easiest. At about 12,000 feet, the steps give way to a continuous slope which can be followed to the summit plateau.

Descend the ascent route.

Route 8	**West Bolam Glacier**
Difficulty:	2
Access:	Whitney or Bolam road
Campsites:	Bolam Creek and numerous morainal steps and benches
Time:	1 to 2 days

Description

The Bolam ("Great One," in the Wintun Indian language) Glacier is very broad and smooth, and easy to climb for a glacier of its size. It is an excellent glacier for newcomers to glacier climbing, or as a first glacier climb on Mt. Shasta. The routes are general and several variations are possible. You can also, escape, if necessary, to the wide ridge to the west at several points. Major difficulties are an obvious long bergschrund and some small crevasses. The access to this route is not the easiest way to the glacier, but if residual snow or other conditions render the northeast approach longer or more difficult, the balance may be tipped in favor of this route. And for some, the rugged beauty of the glacier terminus is its own reward.

The Whitney Glacier base camps can position you for the climb, but it's more advantageous to traverse higher under the Bolam Glacier to a campsite on one of the many morainal shelves. Climb the broad west side of the glacier, passing two very large rock islands on their right sides. From steeper slopes on the glacier's upper reaches, you can attain the summit plateau via mixed climbing to the west, or good, short gullies to the east.

Descend the climbing route.

Route 9	**East Bolam Glacier**
Difficulty:	2
Access:	North Gate Road
Campsites:	North Gate, surrounding forest. The many flat and sandy lateral moraines between the Hotlum and Bolam glaciers also offer excellent campsites and numerous sources of water.
Time:	1 to 2 days

Description

When the North Gate road is open, this is the best access to the Bolam Glacier. The approach hike, or ski, is easy and any of the base camps are comfortable. Choose one of the many excellent high camps described in Route 10 and traverse to the glacier from the vicinity of 10,000 feet. You can also continue west from North Gate, past very large, descending benches to the jumbled moraines at the glacier's foot. Climb to the right of the two large rock islands and from there follow Route 8 to the summit.

Descend the climbing route.

Variation 9	**Bolam Gully**
Difficulty:	3
Time:	1 to 2 days

Description

Climb the long, shallow gully left (E) of the two large rock islands described in the previous routes. The snow in this gully is usually in

Roped climbing on Bolam Glacier

excellent condition, although it can sometimes be icy. When level with the top of the second rock island, you can bear right and follow steep mixed climbing to the summit area, or else traverse east to Route 10 and follow that route to the summit.

Descend either the climbing route or Route 10, depending on conditions and time.

Route 10	**Hotlum-Bolam Ridge**
Difficulty:	2
Access:	North Gate Road
Campsites:	Same as Route 9
Time:	1+ days

Description

The Hotlum-Bolam ridge route is truly a route for all seasons. The access road takes you to an unexpectedly high elevation. The trail through North Gate and the surrounding forest is pleasant, and campsites are numerous with water close at hand. During winter, when parts of the mountain's north side experience a weather "rain-shadow" effect, road access reaches high enough to enable a fairly direct and gentle ski or snowshoe ascent to a suitable base camp. In general, the ridge is not prone to avalanche danger.

Ascend the trail through the North Gate area, the shallow ravine between a large mesa-like lava flow on the left (E), and large, rugged outcroppings on the right (W). Several base camp choices are possible. In early summer, when there is still sufficient snow on the north slopes of the mesa, it may be easily ascended. The top of this formation is a descending series of broad, sandy benches protected from weather and usually offering season-long water in shallow gullies from many accumulated snow drifts. These benches provide some of the most comfortable above-timberline camping anywhere on Shasta.

During late summer, when the mesa's north slopes are devoid of snow, loose talus and scree make a direct ascent to the mesa's top very unpleasant. In that season, continue around the mesa's west shoulder, gain elevation, and cut back to the left (E) on wide talus ramps to a point midway on the series of benches atop the formation. You can also camp a short distance west of the mesa near an unnamed all-season stream, or continue up past a lovely, small waterfall to excellent campsites between 9000 and 10,000 feet.

The climbing route follows broad snow slopes toward the obvious Hotlum-Bolam ridge. If you bear right, you'll find it's steep, but you'll gain the ridge quickly. In good snow conditions, it's better to contour left, skirt the bergschrund on the Hotlum's west lobe, and then follow a broad snow ramp that angles up and to the right to a large, flat platform at 12,800 feet on the ridge. If the lower ridge and the broad ramp are icy, you can traverse left on snow fields that skirt the right side of the middle Hotlum Glacier, then curve around and up to the platform at 12,800 feet. Be prepared for roped glacier travel if you plan to venture onto the Hotlum Glacier. From the platform, the imposing Hotlum headwall looms in full view. Follow a triangular snowfield leading up the ridge to the west toward two obvious rock towers, or "ears," which can be seen from well down the mountain and which are good points of reference. Pass these towers on the right and climb through large broken blocks on the ridge. Follow the ridge to the summit. If wind or ice makes the uppermost ridge undesirable, you can continue past the two "ears" on their right, pass through any of several notches on the ridge, and ascend an easy snow gully hidden on the ridge's west side. This gully may be followed until several short, shallow ribs offer easy return to the ridge just short of the summit. You can also continue climbing in the gully to the hot springs beneath the summit pinnacle.

Descend the climbing route.

Variation 10a Side trip to the Chicago Glacier from the North
Difficulty: 1 to 2
Time: 1 day

Description
From base camp atop the mesa, ascend west a few hundred vertical feet and traverse southeast to this seldom-visited and isolated glacier.

Crossing a crevasse on the Bolam Glacier

AREA: North and Northeast Sides, Hotlum and Wintun Glaciers

Route 11	Hotlum Glacier
Difficulty:	3
Access:	Brewer Creek Trailhead
Campsites:	Brewer Creek, Gravel Creek, moraine lakes and meadows
Time:	2 days

Description

From an impressive rock headwall beginning at nearly 13,000 feet, the Hotlum Glacier descends in a gentle S-turn past 3 spectacular icefalls. At the lowest icefall—a huge broken and convoluted formation just right (N) of a prominent rock prow—the glacier levels out and ends in several acres of fascinating ice ribs. Spread out below this terminus are rugged morainal hummocks and small, hidden lakes. Finally, the headwaters of Gravel Creek and other smaller streams emerge into the red fir and hemlock forests below.

Several fine base camp areas are found in the Brewer and Gravel Creek drainages from which the glacier may be climbed to one of the summit variations. You can also establish a high camp on a prominent rock prow at 11,700 feet below and north of the middle icefall. In spring and early summer the glacier is predominantly smooth from accumulated snow. In late summer and fall, the curved path of the Hotlum Glacier becomes a maze of crevasses, and careful route finding is necessary. At this time the icefalls also come into their best condition for serac climbing.

The climbing route ascends to the right (N) of the lower icefall, then gradually curves upward and left (S) of the middle icefall. Continue upward, again gradually bearing right (N), until reaching the broad upper glacier, which is slightly below and to the left of the upper icefall. At this point, although the slope remains moderate, several crevasses may extend completely across the glacier. In late summer and in times of diminished snow, these abysses can halt easy upward progress. The ridge to the left (S), which becomes most evident above the lower icefall, offers an escape at several points. You can then follow this ridge to the summit. The challenging usual finish is to climb the steep, often icy couloirs just left of the headwall to an

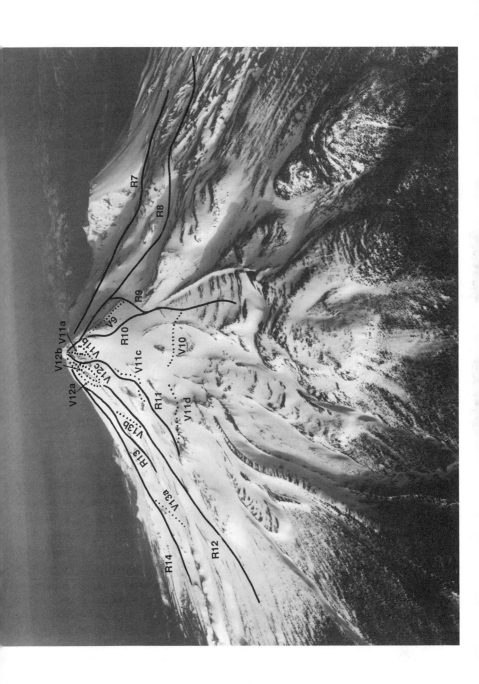

area atop the headwall, and just northeast of the summit pinnacle. From most points on the middle and upper reaches of the Hotlum Glacier, you can also traverse right (N) to join Route 10, the Hotlum-Bolam ridge route.
Descend the climbing route or Route 10.

Variation 11a	Hotlum Glacier Headwall
Difficulty:	3+, Mixed climbing (rock and ice) of maximum difficulty
Time:	2 days

Description

From the bergschrund climb increasingly steep snow to the very apex of the glacier beneath the rock headwall. Three to five rock pitches (some 5.8), depending upon route finding, lead to easier climbing just below the summit pinnacle. The combination of exposure, some loose rock, commitment, and high altitude make this one of the most difficult routes on the mountain.

Variation 11b	Hotlum Headwall Ice Gully
Difficulty:	3+, Mixed climbing (rock and ice) up to very difficult
Time:	2 days

Description

Just right (N) of the obvious headwall in Variation 11a is one of Shasta's longest, steepest ice gullies. In the fall, hard water-ice abounds and this gully is one of the best ice climbs on Mt. Shasta. In summer, scattered snow patches can thinly cover parts of the ice to create deceptively safe but actually very dangerous conditions. The route is easy to follow, but steep, and ends at easier climbing below the summit pinnacle.

Variation 11c	Hotlum Icefalls
Difficulty:	3
Time:	2 days

Descriptions

The three Hotlum icefalls offer Shasta's best and most accessible serac climbing. A careful choice of your base camp or high camp will enable you to enjoy excellent ice climbing only minutes from your tent. The lower icefall, situated at the front of the huge Hotlum amphitheater, conveys a feeling of grandeur, and its mazes of seracs

On the ridge between Bolam and Hotlum glaciers

are exciting to explore. In addition, the broad and gentle terminus glacier below the lower icefall is excellent for beginning glacier and ice training. Plan your high-camp location and climbing activities carefully, because seracs on the middle and lower icefalls may weaken and collapse during warm weather.

Variation 11d Side Trip to the Chicago Glacier from the South

Difficulty: 1 to 2
Time: 1 day

Description

From any of the base camps for the preceding Hotlum Glacier climbing routes, you can traverse north about 1/2 mile with little gain or loss in elevation to the Chicago Glacier. Seldom visited, this glacier has received recent scientific attention and study because of its apparent growth. You can also reach the glacier by a gentle traverse over talus from where the whitebark pine flats meet the undulating morainal hills in the vicinity of Gravel Creek.

Route 12 Hotlum-Wintun Ridge

Difficulty: 2
Access: Brewer Creek Trailhead
Campsites: Same as Route 11
Time: 1+ days

Description

This fine route is one of the most scenic on Shasta's east side, and an excellent alternative to the often-crowded Avalanche Gulch climbs. If the route is followed correctly, almost no glacier technicalities will be encountered. The name "ridge" is a slight misnomer as most of the route follows broad, permanent snowfields located between the Hotlum and the Wintun glaciers. Above 12,400 feet, the ridge separating the glaciers becomes very distinct, and it is one of the variations to the summit.

The Brewer Creek meadow at timberline makes an excellent base camp and offers a very direct start to the climb. Follow the snowfield in the main drainage upward, climbing left (S) of the lower Hotlum icefall and rock cliffs, where incipient crevasses could be troublesome. Continue upward to 12,400 feet, where the ridge becomes distinct. From this high point, choose one of the following summit variations.

Variation 12a Traverse Left (South)
Difficulty: 2
Time: 1+ days

Description

Traverse left (S) to the upper snowfields at the right (N) side of the Wintun Glacier. Pass a solitary, triangular rock island, then climb back right and upward to the rock palisades descending from the summit area. Follow the cliff line to the left (W) until encountering the summit snowfield. Curve around to the north to ascend the summit pinnacle. When there is abundant, stable snow on the route this variation is safe, direct and enjoyable. If there is ice, bad visibility, or concern about nearby crevasses, consider the next variation.

Variation 12b Rock Ridge Direct
Difficulty: 2
Time: 1+ days

Description

Climb directly up the Hotlum-Wintun rock ridge that begins at 12,400 feet. With careful route finding, the ridge is 3rd class. If 4th class sections are encountered, they are usually very short, and avoidable by traversing to easier climbing. In ice, verglas, or bad weather, a rope would be advisable. The ridge ends almost directly at the summit.

Variation 12c	**Traverse Right (North)**
Difficulty:	2 to 3
Time:	1+ days

Description

This third alternative angles right (N) at the ridge break at 12,400 feet and follows a steep snowfield which skirts the left side of the Hotlum headwall. As this snowfield-cum-gully narrows, stay left of a thin rock rib and climb to easy ground at the summit area.

Descending the Eastside Routes

An eastside descent is potentially hazardous, and forethought should be given to all the variables. Generally, what you have just climbed is fresh and familiar in your mind, and for this reason should be the descent of choice.

If key features and landmarks are noted on the ascent, they can be very useful during the descent. If snow conditions change, visibility or weather worsens, or darkness falls, the two snow variations (Variation 12a and Variation 12c) become very dangerous with unexpected dropoffs and/or crevasses not far from the safe route. Wands or flagging should be placed at critical points on the ascent to mark the route. The rock ridge (Variation 12b), although slower going than the snow variations, avoids any serious dropoffs. At 12,400 feet, continue the descent on the broad snowfield.

Route 13	**Wintun Glacier**
Difficulty:	2 to 3
Access:	Brewer Creek Trailhead
Campsites:	Same as Route 11
Time	1+ days

Description

The Wintun Glacier, named for a local Indian tribe, has many different sections. The upper glacier is wide and clean, and from a beginning just below the east face of the summit pinnacle, the east tongue of the glacier descends smoothly to plateaus between Brewer and Ash creeks. The southeast tongue of the glacier pours over a precipitous icefall and into steep Ash Creek canyon. The lower glacier is an interesting maze of crisscrossing crevasses, and the icefall offers fine practice climbing.

You can establish a base camp near Brewer Creek, or one closer to the glacier by traversing south to the highest of three flat hills seen silhouetted on the ridge south of Brewer Creek. From these hills, you can see most of the route, and a descending traverse will take you to the lower glacier. Except for spring and early summer, some talus will be encountered on this traverse—try to look ahead to avoid the loosest sections. Pass the icefall on either side, depending on snow conditions, and on where the least debris from above appears to be falling. Easier climbing on the left side of the glacier leads to the summit snowfield.

Descend the climbing route or Wintun Ridge (R 14).

Variation 13a   Traverse to Wintun Ridge
Difficulty: 2
Time: 1+ days

Description

If conditions on the lower Wintun Glacier and the icefall appear unstable, or debris is raining down from above, you can traverse south out of the canyon to Wintun Ridge. Climb upward on the broad ridge to the summit snowfield, or traverse to the upper Wintun Glacier and follow it to the summit.

Descend the climbing route.

Variation 13b   Brewer Creek Approach to the Wintun Glacier
Difficulty: 2
Time: 1+ days

Description

Using this approach you can avoid the lower Wintun Glacier and its icefall entirely, while gaining the easier middle and upper reaches of the glacier. From the Brewer Creek drainage, follow snowfields upward and to the south. Attain the broad, eastern tongue of the Wintun Glacier and follow it to the upper glacier and the summit snowfield.

Route 14   Wintun Ridge
Difficulty: 1 to 2
Access: Clear Creek trailhead or Brewer Creek (longer)
Campsites: Clear Creek, Pilgrim Creek's many intermittent meadows and springs
Time: 1 day

Ice climbing on Wintun Glacier

Description

This ridge is relatively easy, has excellent views, and, during the right conditions, offers a superb ski descent as fine as any on Mt. Shasta. From base camp above Clear Creek, Cold Creek or Pilgrim Creek, climb the wide, lower ridge by the best snowfields. The middle and upper sections of the route are generally clean and smooth, but avoid dropoffs to either side of the ridge, as well as a small, south tongue of the Wintun Glacier. Attain the summit snowfield at its southeast end and follow it to the summit pinnacle.

Descend the climbing route.

Variation 14   Side Trip to Watkins Glacier
Difficulty: 1 to 2
Time: 1 day

Description

From the 11,000 feet area on Wintun Ridge, a short southward traverse brings you to the Watkins Glacier. This small glacier and cirque are very beautiful, and the detour is well worth the time.

AREA: East and Southeast Sides, Clear Creek, Mud Creek Canyon and Konwakiton Glaciers

The southeast side of Mt. Shasta is distinguished by a very broad, gentle shoulder between the Konwakiton Glacier and the great cleft of Mud Creek canyon, and the Wintun Glacier. This gradual slope was noticed early in Shasta's climbing history, and it became popular because of its ease. This was the way Old Jump Up, the first horse to stand atop Mt. Shasta, made his notable climb in the late 1800s. Evidence of an old trail is often seen in times of light snow. High camps of the early climbers are still found, occasionally complete with neat, small stacks of sun-bleached firewood carried above timberline before the advent of today's ultralight camp stoves.

Route 15	Clear Creek
Difficulty:	1
Access:	Clear Creek trailhead
Campsites:	Same as Route 14
Time:	1 day

Description

From one of several excellent base camp sites between Mud Creek and Clear Creek, the broad, gradual slope of the climbing route is very evident, resembling a gently tilted isosceles triangle. In spring and early summer, abundant snow allows an easy climb. However, the southern exposure causes the snowpack to melt rapidly, leaving unpleasant talus and sand. In late summer you must try to find a route that links snowfields together to bypass most of the talus. At 13,000 feet avoid steep chutes dropping off on either side of the climbing route, to the Konwakiton and the Wintun glaciers. This pleasing route ends on the broad summit snowfield just west of the summit pinnacle.

Descend via the climbing route.

Route 16	Konwakiton Glacier from the East
Difficulty:	3
Access:	Clear Creek trailheads
Campsites:	Same as Route 14
Time:	1+ to 2 days

Description

The Konwakiton ("Muddy One," in the Wintun Indian language) Glacier is one of Shasta's smallest glaciers, extending down only to about 12,000 feet. The glacier lies at the head of Mt. Shasta's most immense gorge, Mud Creek Canyon, and only the imagination can ponder the scale of the geologic and glacial events that shaped this huge chasm. Here is some of the steepest and most rugged terrain on Mt. Shasta.

The best approach to the climbing route is via a traverse from the Clear Creek route. Begin the traverse at an elevation near or above waterfalls emanating from the glacier's foot. Rockfall can be a serious problem on this route: Take great care on the approach, as the sun can soften the rock's frozen mortar from above. A vertical rock ridge divides the glacier; you can pass left of this ridge to gain immediate entrance to the steep icefall, or pass the ridge on its right to avoid the icefall altogether. There are many variations on the glacier—from steep, difficult ice to challenging mixed climbing on rock ribs. The slope of the glacier decreases near its apex. Climb northeast to the summit snowfield and continue to the summit pinnacle.

Descend via the Clear Creek route.

Route 17	**Konwakiton Glacier from the South**
Difficulty:	3
Access:	Same as Route 3
Campsites:	Same as Route 3
Time:	1 to 2 days

Description

From Sargents Ridge you can establish a high camp on the north side of Shastarama Point or at the base of the Mud Creek Glacier. Approach the Konwakiton Glacier from the southwest. The easiest approach will be dictated by current conditions. You can avoid the icefall by climbing steep gullies on the left. When adequate snow cover is present and loose rocks are cemented well in place, it's convenient to traverse below the icefall to direct ascent lines east of the rock ridge dividing the glacier.

Descend via Sargents Ridge.

5 Skiing on Mt. Shasta

Vast glaciers and snowfields, immense vertical drops, and plentiful winter snowfall have long attracted skiers to Mt. Shasta. During winter, skiers of all abilities, as well as snowshoers and winter campers, can find endless opportunities for recreation on the mountain. Even during the height of a storm, enjoyable skiing awaits within the protected forests below timberline. During spring and early summer many of the climbing routes can be combined with an exciting partial or complete descent on skis—beginning from as high as the summit. Favorable snow conditions often allow descents of more than 6000 vertical feet!

In this chapter we describe the range of ski possibilities on Mt. Shasta. Ski mountaineering and all backcountry skiing require knowledge of technique, proper equipment, and the ability to be self-sufficient. Preparation for and experience with various snow conditions, weather conditions, and avalanche dangers should be considered *de rigueur*, as there are no cookbook formulas or shortcuts for avoiding potential dangers and hazards on Mt. Shasta—or on any other mountain. The most crucial hazard that backcountry skiers have to concern themselves with is avalanches. Beginning ski tourers who stick to meadows and gentle slopes in the forest have little to worry about, but when you enter the realm of backcountry skiing and ski mountaineering, you enter the realm of potential avalanches. Avalanche forecasting is a fascinating subject, and skiers are urged to seek out instruction. Two superb texts on the subject are *The ABC of Avalanche Safety*, by Ed LaChapelle, and *Avalanche Safety for Skiers and Climbers*, by Tony Daffern. In addition, the U.S. Forest Service has prepared an excellent video, *Avalanche Awareness*.

Because Mt. Shasta receives plenty of snowfall, most (but not all) avalanches on Shasta are "direct-action" avalanches, which occur during storms or soon after, as a result of new snow loading the slopes. Current snow and weather conditions can always be obtained locally in order to help you plan and prepare for an outing. Phone numbers for 24-hour weather and climbing information messages are listed at the end of the "Weather" Chapter in this book.

Ski routes can be described only in general. Terrain, snow conditions, weather, visibility, and potential avalanche danger vary seasonally, and even daily. Certain ski routes and tours are best at certain seasons, as indicated below.

Skiing on Mt. Shasta may be divided into four general categories:

I. A ski descent in conjunction with one of the climbing routes. This may be the conclusion of a summit climb, or skiing itself may be the objective.

II. Highway winter access. The best access for beginner/intermediate skiers, and access to some selected advanced runs, is Everitt Memorial Highway on Shasta's southwest side. This highway is plowed regularly as far as Bunny Flat.

III. Ski-in base camps. Many excellent skiing areas require a long skiing approach, but a base camp in a wilderness setting makes the effort worthwhile. Access to such places via gravel roads varies with the season.

IV. Lift-serviced and cross country ski areas. Mount Shasta Ski Park and Castle Lake Cross Country Ski Area both operate on a regular schedule throughout the winter.

In addition, we describe:

V. Castle Lake highway access, Mt. Eddy, and the west side of Strawberry Valley.

VI. Mt. Shasta Ski Circumnavigation.

Key to Ski Routes

Access: The best approach, road or otherwise, at various seasons.

Season: The time of year for the best skiing of the route or area.

Level: Degree of difficulty of skiing in area. (We've tried to balance the ratings between cross-country/telemark and downhill equipment. On the more difficult descents, the skiing will tend to be a little harder than the rating if you're using cross-country gear; a little easier if you're using randonee or downhill gear.)

* means previously recorded avalanche activity

I. Skiing the Climbing Routes

Many of the climbing routes on Shasta are excellent ski routes as well. With a little added ski equipment and preparation, these climbing routes can become exciting ski descents. Access, route descriptions and other information appear in detail in the climbing chapter. The following is a sequential listing, clockwise around Mt. Shasta from Avalanche Gulch, of the best climb/ski routes, along with special comments as they apply.

Route 1*   **Traditional John Muir/Avalanche Gulch**

Season: Spring to early summer
Level: Advanced

Avalanche Gulch, the immense, open bowl on Shasta's southwest flank, offers nearly unlimited skiing possibilities. For those desiring a descent from the actual summit, this route has the most consistent snow conditions, although the reaches above the Red Banks often have poor quality and/or sparse snow cover.

Variation 1a*   Left of Heart
Season: Spring to early summer
Level: Advanced

Telemark skiing in lower Avalanche Gulch

This steep variation avoids the Red Banks when they're lacking enough skiable snow. If cornices near the top of the Red Banks are passable, this run is one of the most exciting on Mt. Shasta.

Route 2*   Old Ski Bowl

Season: Spring to early summer
Level: Intermediate and Advanced

This bowl is pleasant and scenic. It's impractical to ski this route starting from above 10,000 feet because of steep rock cliffs, but the route can be connected by traverse to Route 1 for maximum vertical drop.

Route 4*   Green Butte Ridge

Season: Late winter to early spring
Level: Intermediate and advanced

This ridge offers access to several other bowls, and also can be connected to Route 1.

Variation 5*   West Face Gully

Season: Spring to early summer
Level: Advanced to expert

This steep gully is a candidate for the "extreme" category, but soft, spring-type snow can bring it into the range of many skiers.

Route 6*   Cascade Gulch

Season: Spring to early summer
Level: Intermediate and advanced

This very delightful, curving, open bowl allows a moderate, traversing descent from Shastina to Horse Camp.

Route 7*   Whitney Glacier

Season: Late winter to early summer
Level: Intermediate and advanced

With adequate snow cover the vast lower glacier is excellent for skiing, and it provides access for winter and spring ascents of the upper glacier.

Taking a break on ridge above Green Butte

Variation 7b*   Whitney-Bolam Ridge
Season: Late winter to early spring
Level: Advanced
This ridge is an excellent ski descent when there is ample snow.

Route 8*   Bolam Glacier from the northwest
Season: Late winter to early spring
Level: Intermediate and advanced
The Bolam's lack of serious crevasses makes it Shasta's best glacier to ski.

Route 9*   Bolam Glacier from the northeast
Season: Late winter to early spring
Level: Intermediate and advanced

Variation 9a*   Bolam Gully
Season: Spring
Level: Advanced to expert
The Bolam Gully is another ski descent route in the "extreme" category.

Route 10*   Hotlum-Bolam Ridge
Season: Spring to early summer
Level: Advanced
The ridge itself is not consistently skiable because of too many exposed rocks, but the snowfields on either side of the ridge stay in skiable condition remarkably long into summer and can be connected in many ways for superb ski descents.

Route 11*   Hotlum Glacier
Season: Spring
Level: Advanced
The Hotlum Glacier is not especially steep, but it can be difficult to ski because of the large icefalls and a maze of crevasses. However, careful route finding will reach excellent ski terrain.

Route 12*   **Hotlum-Wintun Ridge**
Season: Late winter to spring
Level: Intermediate and advanced
   This is usually one of the longest-lasting snow slopes on Shasta, often skiable through the summer, or until the sun cups become too large.

Route 13*   **Wintun Glacier**
Season: Spring to early summer
Level: Advanced
   The upper reaches of the glacier are excellent skiing, and they can be connected with Route 12 for a long descent.

   The following two routes are spring favorites and offer broad, wide skiing terrain with moderate slopes.

Route 14*   **Wintun Ridge**
Season: Late winter to spring
Level: Intermediate and advanced

Route 15*   **Clear Creek**
Season: Late winter to spring
Level: Intermediate and advanced

II. Winter Access: Everitt Memorial Highway

   In 1912 local citizens decided that a wagon road from the town of Sisson to Horse Camp was necessary to promote tourism. Work was begun on the popularly called "Mt. Shasta Snowline Highway" in 1927 and completed all the way to Panther Meadows by 1940. In 1934 the yet-uncompleted highway was renamed "The John Samuel Everitt Memorial Highway" in honor of the supervisor of the Shasta National Forest who had died on August 25, 1934, fighting a fire on Shasta's southern flanks. Paved in 1956, the road is now known as Everitt Memorial Highway. Complete with milestones and elevation markers along its 14-mile length, the highway was plowed regularly throughout the winter during the heyday of the Mt. Shasta Ski Bowl. Since the Ski Bowl ceased operation in 1978, Siskiyou County road crews now plow only to the 11-mile point, at Bunny Flat. The remaining 3 miles of the road remain beneath snow, usually through June, but the road is still easy to follow and it makes for an enjoyable ski tour. The early designers of the highway had probably never seen skis when they began planning the road, but their design was fortuitous: Everitt Memorial Highway allows access to some of the finest and most varied skiing found anywhere on Shasta. There is parking at Bunny Flat (11 miles), Sand Flat (10 miles) and the Wagon Camp turnout, or switchback (7 miles).

The following areas are arranged in descending progression along Everitt Memorial Highway from the old Ski Bowl, and continue clockwise around the mountain.

Unplowed Everitt Highway, Bunny Flat to Old Ski Bowl
Level: Beginner and intermediate
Other activity: Snowshoeing
The gently contoured Everitt Highway, under snow its last 3 miles from Bunny Flat to Panther Meadows, is easy to follow as it winds through stately Shasta red fir trees. This is an excellent short tour with an easy return.

Old Ski Bowl*
Level: Intermediate and advanced
In the days of the old ski area, the two sides of this large, open cirque were identified as the "West Bowl" and the "East Bowl." The west bowl, adjacent to precipitous Green Butte, is steep and challenging; the east bowl is more rolling and gentle.

Tour to Squaw Valley*
Level: Intermediate and advanced
Other activity: Snow camping
From the bottom of the Ski Bowl cirque, traverse east through an obvious notch in Sargents Ridge. Continue through The Gate, the pass between Red Butte and the mountain, and into the beautiful

hemlock forests of Squaw Valley. Continue to ski farther east for outstanding winter views of the Konwakiton Glacier and Mud Creek Canyon.

Panther Meadows
Level: Beginner and Intermediate
Other activities: Snowshoeing, snow camping
Below the old Ski Bowl and just west of Gray Butte are the gentle rolling hills and forest of Panther Meadows. Close proximity to parking at Bunny Flat makes this a desirable destination for snow camping or ski touring. A pleasant side trip, all downhill, is to ski 2 1/2 miles cross-country south to Mt. Shasta Ski Park. Pre-arrange a shuttle or pick-up for this variation.

Wagon Camp
Level: Intermediate
From Panther Meadows traverse west, parallel to and below Everitt Memorial Highway, through forest and open slopes. Finish at the Wagon Camp switchback, a convenient shuttle point.

Gray Butte Northwest Face*
Level: Advanced
Gray Butte is the steep hill bordering the southeast edge of Panther Meadows. The best approach to ski the north face of the butte is via the ridge on the left (N) of the north face.

Powder Bowl and Sun Bowl*
Level: Intermediate and advanced
Powder Bowl and Sun Bowl are the two very distinct, above-timberline bowls between Green Butte and Bunny Flat, Sun Bowl being the westernmost. The easiest approach is via Green Butte Ridge from Bunny Flat. The lower parts of these bowls may be reached from several points along the unplowed Everitt Memorial Highway track. These two bowls offer some of the finest early spring snow on Shasta.

Skiing in the lower reaches of Powder Bowl

Broadway*
Level: Intermediate and advanced
   The wide lower half of Green Butte Ridge is called Broadway. The skiing here is excellent when sufficient snow covers some very large rocks.

Bunny Flat Area
Level: Beginner and intermediate
Other activities: Snowshoeing, snow camping
   Bunny Flat, at the end of the plowed part of Everitt Memorial Highway, is parking area, staging area and hub for ski tours to every direction.
   The most popular half-day ski tour on Mt. Shasta is undoubtedly the short jaunt to the Sierra Club cabin at Horse Camp. Head north a few hundred yards, passing through an obvious break in the near ridge to the west, then gradually climb northwest. Yellow metal triangles on trees mark this ski trail. A metal rain tower marks the

two-thirds point of the route. The cabin is always unlocked, and it makes a wonderful winter base camp or a place for lunch and socializing.

You can also ski to Sand Flat or Wagon Camp from Bunny Flat, shuttle back up Everitt Memorial Highway, and repeat the run.

Horse Camp Area and Beyond*
Level: Beginner, intermediate, advanced
Other activity: Snowshoeing, snow camping

The Sierra Club cabin is an excellent base camp for skiing in the cabin's own backyard: the immense Avalanche Gulch basin. North of the cabin are advanced-level bowls, Cascade Gulch and Hidden Valley.

SPECIAL EXTRA: Diller Canyon*
Season: Spring to summer
Level: Advanced to expert

Diller Canyon is the very large and unmistakable cleft in the west face of Shastina. During the winter, strong, jet-stream-velocity north winds carry enormous quantities of snow from Shastina's flanks to the lee (S) side of the canyon, where it remains throughout the summer. Although this is not a particularly worthy climbing route, as a ski descent route it is one of the longest and most exciting on Shasta. For the expert skier, this one should not be missed.

Access to Diller Canyon can be a problem because of rough dirt roads; a truck with ample clearance or a four-wheel-drive vehicle is necessary. Drive up Everitt Memorial Highway 3.6 miles to a dirt road on the left marked BLACK BUTTE TRAILHEAD. Follow this dirt road 0.8 mile, then turn east on another dirt road. Follow this road as it curves north, then west, then north again as high as possible along Shastina's flank. Disrepair and constant additions to this maze of logging roads cause access directions to change yearly. If in doubt, follow the line of least resistance to as high as possible; the hike to Diller Canyon is scenic and not very long.

Horse Camp to McBride Springs*

Level: Intermediate and advanced

This is one of the best descents on the southwest slope of Shasta. From the Sierra Club cabin, traverse north $1/4$ mile and follow the slopes on the south side of Cascade Gulch until you meet Everitt Memorial Highway near the McBride Springs campground. This ski descent is more than 4 miles long and drops more than 4000 vertical feet.

Sand Flat Area

Level: Beginner and intermediate
Other activities: Snowshoeing, snow camping

Sand Flat is a beautiful open meadow with postcard-perfect views of upper Mt. Shasta. The meadow can be reached by a $1/2$ mile ski-in over one of two easy-to-follow snow-covered roads. There is a parking area at the upper road (10.2 milepost and SAND FLAT sign), and another at the lower road, about 0.6 mile down Everitt Memorial Highway. The upper road is nearly flat; the lower one is steeper but more fun to ski down. The Forest Service has placed signs on the trees to mark several easy scenic tours within the area. A cross country ski trail map for Sand Flat is available at the Mt. Shasta Ranger Station.

Red Fir Flat

Level: Beginner
Other activities: Snowshoeing, snow camping

Located just below the lower road to Sand Flat, the gentle terrain of Red Fir Flat is especially suited for beginners.

Through avalanche swath en route to Horse Camp

III. Ski-in Base Camps: Wilderness Skiing

A true winter delight is skiing into a plateau or a protected valley, establishing a comfortable base camp, and then skiing untracked terrain during wilderness' most magical time. Mt. Shasta has several such "secret" spots. Keep in mind that the only limiting factor is your imagination. A guidebook may be useful, but a sense of adventure is the key. A little extra effort may be required to get to the chosen areas, but the reward is wilderness skiing at its finest. Following are a few of the best areas.

The north and northeast sides of Shasta sometimes experience unusual winter weather effects: a cold stillness descends and dry powder snow remains in the valleys and the gullies for weeks on end. When the Military Pass and Andesite roads are open, access to the North Gate, and the Inconstance, Gravel and Brewer Creek drainages is afforded. Excellent snow is usually found here.

Similar excellent snow conditions can often be found on Shasta's east flanks, but access depends upon how far you can first drive up Pilgrim Creek Road. A long ski-in to base camp is usually necessary, but the terrain is gentle. The Cold, Pilgrim, Ash and Clear Creek drainages offer the best snow.

IV. Lift-Serviced and Commercial Ski Areas

Mt. Shasta has a long history of downhill skiing, going back more than 50 years to the "Mount Shasta Snowmen" ski club. Snowmans Hill, at the crest of Highway 89 between the towns of McCloud and Mount Shasta, was a 90-meter ski jump considered to be one of the best ski-jumping hills in North America during the 1930s. Southern Pacific Railroad had special weekend ski trains from the San Francisco Bay area to Snowmans Hill, and several ski-jumping championships were held there. When Everitt Memorial Highway was completed in 1940, several plans for ski lifts on the mountain were proposed. These different proposals included, at various times, lifts from the town of Mount Shasta to the top of the mountain! The old Mt. Shasta Ski Bowl, located above Panther Meadow, operated from 1958 until 1978. The Mt. Shasta Ski Park, below Panther Meadow and Gray Butte, opened in 1985, is presently the one commercial ski area on Mt. Shasta. It has two triple chairs and a surface lift, complete lodge facilities, ski school and night skiing—all on groomed trails serving beginners to experts. In addition, it has a telemark program and instruction.

The Mt. Shasta Ski Park also offers a summer program that includes scenic chairlift rides, mountain biking, guided nature hikes, natural history exhibits, and various special events.

V. The Eddys, Castle Lake and Beyond

The "Eddys" refers to the mountains across the valley to the west of Mt. Shasta, dominated by 9025-foot Mt. Eddy. The Klamath, Siskiyou and Scott mountains all meet in this area, which is very old geologically compared to Mt. Shasta. If you're adventurous, spectacular mountain scenery, hidden backcountry bowls, and possibilities for exploration abound in the Eddys. The Castle Lake Road, snowplowed as far as the cross-country ski area, is a good departure point. A special backcountry ski-touring map for this area is available at the Fifth Season outdoor shop in Mount Shasta; other maps are available at the District Ranger office.

VI. Mt. Shasta Ski Circumnavigation

Mt. Shasta's quintessential ski tour is for advanced and expert backcountry skiers. The general rule of thumb is to remain near timberline, although many variations are possible. A clockwise direction of travel is best, usually starting from the Sierra Club cabin at Horse Camp. This starting point is especially advised because if the nearby northwest flanks of Shastina have been scoured of snow by the wind, as they often have been, skiers can easily backtrack to the cabin. A counterclockwise course could bring you to the northwest side of Shastina several days after beginning the trip, with no convenient escape route if lack of snow prevented a skiing return to the cabin. Some additional caveats: You can cross Ash Creek canyon either above or below the falls. Going above the falls entails elevation gain, but offers an easy canyon crossing. Going low offers the protection of the forest, but a steeper canyon to cross. Mud Creek canyon should be crossed in the vicinity of its confluence with Clear Creek. Any higher crossing is steeper and longer; a lower crossing means additional gorges to contend with and considerable elevation to regain.

This circumnavigation is an unforgettable ski trip on a great mountain. Needless to say, careful preparations, heavy-duty equipment, and self-sufficiency are necessary. You should plan on 4 or 5 days for the ski circumnavigation of Mt. Shasta.

6 Water Activities

Mt. Shasta is a gigantic, porous mass of volcanic material that absorbs water from glaciers, surface snow and rain like a huge sponge. The porous rock within the mountain's mass acts like a giant reservoir—an aquifer—slowly releasing its water through a number of springs surrounding the mountain. The temperature of the water is constant throughout the year, and the quantity and quality of the water are very high. The Sacramento, Shasta and McCloud rivers are all directly fed from the Mt. Shasta aquifer.

Boating, Rafting and Kayaking

The Sacramento and McCloud rivers, within Mt. Shasta's watershed influence, will give you excellent whitewater thrills throughout the spring and summer. The McCloud stretch begins at the lower falls in Fowler's campground east of the town of McCloud off Highway 89. The river passes through lush, old-growth forests and ends at Lake McCloud, where a boat ramp facilitates take-out and shuttles. Plan for a full day. The McCloud is not open to commercial rafting companies or outfitters, so you'll have to tackle this gem without help.

The upper Sacramento River canyon offers a cornucopia of exciting whitewater runs from Dunsmuir to Lake Shasta. There are numerous points for put-in and take-out, and you'll find several surprise views of Mt. Shasta to be unforgettable. Plan for up to a full day. The Sacramento River is open to commercial river outfitters; you can obtain current listings and brochures of these concessionaires from an outdoor shop or the district ranger offices.

There are four other major rivers nearby, and although not within the Mt. Shasta watershed, they offer some of the finest whitewater in the west. The Klamath, Scott, Salmon and Trinity rivers offer excellent boating, from Class II (easiest) to Class V (expert), on runs as short as a few hours or as long as several days. Commercial river rafters and professional guides are available for all of these rivers, and you can obtain their listings from the various district rangers and outdoor shops.

The McCloud River

7 Mountain Biking

Mt. Shasta's network of logging roads offers vast backcountry cycling opportunities. To be sure, many roads run through ugly logged areas, and some have frustrating sandy sections, but locals have found that mountain bikes open up a new realm of exploration and exercise on Shasta. The included 7.5' topographic map in this book and the surrounding USGS 7.5' quads are the best guides to the miles and miles of riding. Here we suggest a couple of the more rewarding trips.

Mountain bikes may be rented at various shops in Mount Shasta. Bike trail maps and route-guides are also available. As in any federal wilderness area, all mechanical transport is barred from Mt. Shasta Wilderness. Shasta's hiking trails are generally too sandy to tempt bicyclists anyway.

Forest Road 31

From Mt. Shasta Ski Park this main forest road runs east on a good surface and curves north to the east side of the mountain. Here you can join the road to the Clear Creek or to the Brewer Creek trailhead, described in the "Hiking" Chapter. These also make good rides, from Highway 89 east of McCloud.

The Northern Arc

This adventurous tour follows roads around the north side of Shasta, via Military Pass. Although at least one party has completed the trip in one very long day, depending on the end point this is generally a 2-day venture. Most riders will want to avoid midsummer heat on this ride. From Highway 97 follow the Military Pass road (directions under the North Gate hike) over Military Pass and continue southeast onto Road 19. This leads into Road 31, which you can follow to the city of Mount Shasta via Mt. Shasta Ski Park, or you can head southeast on Road 41N15 (as directed, in reverse, under the Clear Creek hike) to the Pilgrim Creek Road and on to Highway 89 east of McCloud. From Highway 97 to Highway 89 the journey is about 35 miles.

Co-author Selters biking on Shasta

8 The Flora and Fauna

Mt. Shasta stands as a recently created "island" of mountain habitat. For plants, Shasta apparently is a tough habitat because even though Shasta's slopes receive 20-40 *feet* of snow each winter, most of the slopes are surprisingly dry, even desertlike. Compared to its neighbor volcanoes, Lassen Peak and the Crater Lake volcano, noticeably fewer plant species grow on Shasta. To understand the unusual and relatively spartan biota of Mt. Shasta, we first have to understand the unusual substrate and the climate.

The Substrate

From a hydrologist's point of view, Mt. Shasta is indeed a hollow mountain. The volcanic debris that makes up the mountain is extremely porous, and even the overlying forest soils are too sandy to retain the precious snowmelt. Therefore a large percentage of Mt. Shasta's heavy snowpacks percolates into underground aquifers, and even sizable streams disappear into the ground before they reach low elevations. For the surrounding cities, rivers and lakes, Shasta is a veritable fountain, because the subterranean waters gush out in cold, copious springs all around its perimeter. The plants on the mountain itself, however, are left high and dry. Although other Cascade volcanoes have this percolation effect, none have such extensive dry slopes as Shasta because none have as much porous lava, and those farther north are more covered with glaciers.

The Climate

At its lookout over both the southern Cascades and California's Central Valley, Mt. Shasta receives an alternation of storms from the north and fair weather from the south. In general, the pattern shifts with the seasons, fair weather dominating in summer and frequent storms blasting the mountain during winter. "Unseasonable surprises" visit every season, though, bringing occasional midsummer storms and long winter sunny spells. Although copious precipitation and sun seem to add up to serendipity for plants, these dramatic "surprises" often make life hard for them.

Mt. Shasta also stands at (and helps form) an east-west climatic divide. On the west, the Pacific Ocean moderates temperatures and pumps moisture into the storms. On the east, the Great Basin contributes drier inland air to Shasta, so the mountain's eastern slopes have colder, drier winters than its western slopes.

These influences are the raw material of Mt. Shasta's climate, but to the life on its slopes the more powerful influence is the way the mountain's mass and its altitude rework weather. Most important among altitude's influences is that when a stormy air mass hits Mt. Shasta and rises upslope, the air expands and cools. Cooler air can hold less moisture, so as storms rise up the mountain they dump ever more rain and snow, up to a point.

Thus, higher elevations have colder temperatures, and they receive more snow and rain—up to a point. Above 8-9000 feet, storms drop *less* precipitation because the rising air has given up most of its moisture below, and because the thin air at high altitude in general is very dry. Therefore, a typical winter storm on Mt. Shasta will dump increasing rain up to 3-4000 feet, and increasingly heavy snow up to perhaps 9000 feet. Above that we find moderate snowfall, usually accompanied by screaming winds.

The Flora

On Shasta, the climatic effects of increasing elevation are so significant that the character of the flora changes completely with elevation. Because Mt. Shasta rises as a nearly symmetrical "island" of increasing altitude, an overly simple model of its ecology would depict concentric rings of different floral groupings circling the mountain each at its favored elevation. Of course, such variables as species' different tolerances and the complex effects of slope aspect and drainage make such a model only modestly accurate, but the concept is instructive.

Low on Shasta, up to 5500 feet or so, plants find hot, dry summers and cool, rainy winters. Most of these lower slopes are covered with chaparral, dominated by greenleaf manzanita and tobacco brush, a ceanothus. Other chaparral shrubs include oaklike chinquapin, buck-brush ceanothus, antelope brush and Western chokecherry. From a distance the chaparral appears as a pleasant green rug reaching up the mountain, and throughout spring and summer the shrubs erupt with a plethora of flowers and the buzzing of nectar-drunk bees. Among the shrubs grow gardens of flowering herbs, including penstemons, gilia, and the queen of Shasta's flowers, the endangered Shasta lily.

The riot of chaparral growth did not cover the area without help, however. It has taken over since loggers cleared the native forests. In 1898 the biologist C.H. Merriam wrote, "Shasta rises from a forested region and the mountain itself is continuously forest-covered up to an altitude of 7500 feet or 8000 feet." Photographs and other accounts show that the logging actually started before Merriam's studies, but whenever it started, these native woods were dominated by ponderosa pine on the lower slopes and white fir higher up. The chaparral no doubt grew in scattered clearings, and after the logging, the aggressive, sun-loving brush took over.

Douglas phlox

The chaparral is now very dense, and the shrubs' shade hinders their own seedlings. Pine seedlings, however, need shade, so in theory the forest will eventually overcome the chaparral—assuming no fires or other new disturbances. Since the Great Depression the Forest Service has been planting orderly rows of hybridized ponderosa pine among Shasta's chaparral, in an effort to speed the return of marketable timber.

Above 5500 feet, cooler temperatures, heavier precipitation, and greater distance from logging mills allow conifers to gradually become dominant. Towering over the shrubs you see the long-needled branches of ponderosa pine, the "Christmas tree" spires of white fir and Douglas-fir, the splayed branches of sugar pine and the cone rosettes of knobcone pine. This forest community grows richest on Shasta's southern slopes; sparser trees and more brush characterize the drier northwest wide. On the northeast side, a rather scraggly forest of lodgepole pines struggles with the Great Basin influence of cold, dry winters.

Above 6000 feet, almost all precipitation comes as winter snows, and here begins the domination of one majestic species of tree, Shasta red fir. This tree is very closely related to red fir of the Sierra, and to noble fir, which mostly grows farther north in the Cascades. Like its cousins, Shasta red fir grows curved combs of blue-green needles, and furrowed maroon bark over stolid, unbranched trunks. However, unlike red fir proper, Shasta red fir has cones with pointed, papery bracts hanging from each seed envelope, and its needles and bark differ subtly from those of noble fir.

In its other habitats Shasta red fir grows with one of these cousins, but on Mt. Shasta it rings the mountain in an essentially exclusive forest between 6500 feet and 8000 feet. Another curiosity of Shasta red fir is that to the south the bracted subspecies isn't found for 300 miles, until you reach the southern Sierra. This disjointed distribution probably dates from the glacial epochs, when glaciers and a snowy climate likely eliminated the Shasta red fir from most of the Sierra.

Mt. Shasta's porous, dry soils force the firs to keep their distance from one another, so these montane forests of Shasta offer wonderfully open walking and skiing. In the dry duff you notice scattered herbs like white-veined wild ginger, mountain violet and the delicate pink steer's head. In recent decades logging has eaten into the Shasta red-fir forest, leaving precious little forest.

Almost synonymous with the snowy Cascades is the delicate nodding tip of the mountain hemlock, and moist pockets in Shasta's montane forests do foster this graceful tree. In upper Squaw Valley diminutive hemlocks dominate; just above, on the east slopes of Gray Butte, some tall, stout hemlocks compare in stature with red firs. Isolated groves and individuals of mountain hemlock surprise one throughout the montane forests, and up to timberline at 8500 feet.

Mountain hemlock with nodding tip

It's in the openings in the montane forest that the aridity of Shasta's soils is most obvious. At these snowy elevations elsewhere in California and Oregon you'd expect to see green carpets of sedges, grasses and wildflowers, but on Shasta the meadows are sandy —although certainly not without their own floral beauty. Generally one of two flower shrubs dominates, either silver lupine with its purple flower-spikes, or Bloomer's goldbush with its haphazard, thin yellow petals. Pennyroyal usually wafts its mint-resins through these clearings, and even a casual overview finds paintbrush, phlox, mountain buckwheat, arnica or pussy paws adding summer color between the two dominant shrubs.

Shasta's dry clearings host a few fairly rare plants. Shasta arnica grows only in the Shasta and Crater Lake areas, and Shasta knotweed grows only a little more widely, as far as the northern Sierra. *Phacelia cookei*, a member of the waterleaf family named after Shasta's premier botanist, Dr. William Bridge Cook, grows only on the lower north slopes of Mt. Shasta. The floral relationships of these plants suggest that they have evolved in recent millenia in response to the sandy, dry conditions.

Lusher meadows are found on Shasta, almost exclusively along the profuse springs of Panther and Squaw Valley creeks. Sogginess from these springs keeps the forest at bay, while rushes, sedges and mountain heather flourish. One rare plant, Shasta bluebell, grows only at the springs at the head of Panther Creek and in the Trinity Alps.

Alpine buckwheat

Krummholz whitebark pines

Above about 8000 feet red firs and other montane vegetation diminish rapidly. Here you come to timberline, that magical place where only the most ascetic trees live a tenuous existence facing bitter cold, biting winds, late-lying snow, and intense radiation. Although occasional Shasta red firs and mountain hemlocks find niches near timberline, *the* timberline tree on Shasta is the whitebark pine.

The cold winters and late-lying snows on Shasta's north and east slopes offer whitebarks ideal conditions, for here, especially, the tree forms extensive "parklands," forests, even, with individuals reaching 30-60 feet tall, and scattered specimens that rival the largest whitebarks ever measured. It appears that the whitebarks do so well here partly because on Shasta's colder north and east sides the red firs reach only to about 7500 feet, leaving the pines more lenient habitat. But even the proudest whitebarks reach skyward with twisted and wretched limbs, the naked and bleached relics of dead growth given up to the elements. It seems that whitebark pines aren't exactly *adapted* to high mountain environments—they're just more enduring.

Higher than about 8500 feet the whitebarks are dwarfed, huddling close together in thickets often no more than a couple of feet high. Curiously, these *krummholz* ("twisted wood") thickets grow highest along Shasta's exposed ridgecrests, up to 9500 feet, where winter snows melt early and allow a long growing season. The risk of such exposed perches is that winters with little snow leave the needles open to icy, blasting winds; after the 1987-88 drought winter, many timberline whitebarks on Shasta showed extensive die-back.

Growing among the whitebarks, and to even higher elevations, are some perennial wildflowers. These hardy plants are more fully *adapted* to the alpine life, sucking moisture from the stony earth that to most plants has long since dried up. Although porous Shasta never allows luxuriant alpine growth, Gray's campion, alpine buckwheat, Shasta knotwood, spreading phlox, Lyall's lupine and others splash color across high, sandy slopes. Probably the most ubiquitous flower is the showy white windflower, which nods over ash and talus fields alike. Talus also shelters "softer" plants like mountain heather, alpine sorrel and timberline phacelia.

The toughest of all Shasta's high flowers is Jacob's Ladder, a rather tender-looking herb whose snow-white blossoms reportedly grow in lonely rock crevices over 13,000 feet. Its vermiform (wormlike) leaves are thick, spongy and finely hairy to store nutrients and retain water.

Life on Shasta has gone to almost miraculous lengths in environments even more extreme. Colorful lichens crust over rocks nearly to the summit. In summer you might notice a pink tint to the snow, conferred by *Chlamydomonas nivalis*, snow algae. Incredibly, another alga has been identified right in the mud of Shasta's summit hot springs. Withstanding temperatures up to 135° and an acidity (pH of 1) many times stronger than vinegar, *Cyanidium caldarium* somehow sustains itself in the fumarole on moisture, minerals and sunlight.

The Fauna

Birds

Birdwatchers may spy up to 100 species of birds on Mt. Shasta, some living year-round on the mountain, some spending springs and summers here to nest, and some just passing through. Here we introduce the most commonly seen species.

During spring and summer the chaparral practically explodes with birdlife, songbirds darting all the daylight hours to feed on the abundant seeds, nectar and insects. You're most likely to see sparrows, warblers, towhees, bluebirds, solitaires and flycatchers—here to breed and rear young, to alight on branches and proclaim territory, bringing a trilling cacophony to Shasta's lower slopes.

In the forests, by comparison, the (merely) numerous birds seem to call down quiet hallways between the big trees. Most commonly one hears the ringing twitters or (in spring) the winsome mating whistles of the mountain chickadee. This bandit-faced bird gleans insects from red-fir boughs. Other calls echoing through the fir forests include the nasal "tin horn" notes of red-breasted nuthatches, the long warbled songs of various Emphidonax flycatchers, and the screeches and cries of two bold cousins, the Steller jay and the gray jay. Woodpeckers drum on the firs, both to announce territory and to drill for insects. Most commonly one sees hairy woodpeckers and white-headed woodpeckers, Nightfall in the forest often brings the haunting calls of a great horned owl.

Among the whitebark pines Clark nutcrackers seem to dominate, probably due as much to their loud, brash demeanor as to their sheer numbers. Another jay-relative, the Clark nutcracker gathers whitebark-pine nuts, eating some off the trees, and storing many for later.

If you wear red in open areas, you'll likely attract hummingbirds, who hope you're a floral nectar source. Both Anna's and rufous hummingbirds make summer stopovers on Shasta to gather nectar before returning in late summer to tropical climes.

Raptors occasionally soar over Shasta, scanning the slopes for rodents and reptiles. Most commonly a binocular fix will show the raptor to be a red-tailed hawk, although golden eagles range over the mountain as well, especially over the eastern slopes. A smaller, fast-flying raptor will probably be either a Cooper's hawk or a sharp-shinned hawk.

The lively little birds of Shasta's alpine slopes are finches. Rosy finches (gray-crowned variety) roam to any elevations they please, scooping insects from the glaciers and often chirping to climbers. Mt. Shasta is California's only known nesting site for the coastal Hepburn's rosy finch. Cassin's finches also twitter around treeline and above, snagging bugs off whitebarks.

Mammals

Although encounters with mammals on Shasta are rather rare, numerous signs like tracks, scats, burrows and middens hint that mammals are common. Most common are the small herbivores, the rodents that feed on seeds, stems and leaves.

The dainty chipmunks have black and white "racing strips" running down their backs and across their eyes. Most chipmunks on Shasta are yellow-pine chipmunks. They share the chaparral and forests up to about 7000 feet with a similarly striped "squirrel," the golden mantled-ground squirrel. This animal lacks the stripes on its face, and its plumper build shows that it stores fat for a winter hibernation. The slender chipmunk, on the other hand, stores a cache of food to fuel its activities during winter's warm spells.

Shasta's common tree squirrel is the lively Douglas squirrel. One never goes far in the red-fir groves without hearing this rusty-olive animal's long, shrilling calls, or its comical *phews* that punctuate its every movement. Shasta is also home to northern flying squirrels, although very few people witness this animal's nighttime glides from tree to tree.

You might flush one of two rabbit species on Shasta. If the ears are particularly long, it is a black-tailed hare; if not, a snowshoe hare. Black-tailed hares tend to live below 7000 feet, while snowshoe hares can be seen up in the whitebark's territory.

The best-known large herbivore on Shasta is the black-tailed deer. These animals migrate between the chaparral and forest zones with the seasons. They especially enjoy new growth, which emerges progressively up the mountain during spring, notably ceanothus and new fir needles.

Canadian elk used to roam on Mt. Shasta, but Muir wrote that by 1918 this animal had been hunted from the mountain. However, a herd based down the Sacramento River Canyon has apparently been ranging onto Shasta, and Selters has found tracks in spring snow on the east slopes of Gray Butte.

Predators

Coyotes, foxes and badgers all feed on squirrels, mice, chipmunks and gophers. Coyotes range all over Shasta, even up to the whitebarks. The gray fox tends to stay in the midelevation forests and the chaparral, mixing a diet of rodents with manzanita berries. The red fox is a larger animal that roams subalpine areas, usually meadows. In years past red foxes were seen around Squaw Valley and Panther Meadow, but it may be that increasing numbers of people visiting these meadows have driven them away.

Badgers are low-slung, powerful animals that root out rodents from underground. A burrow on Shasta anywhere below 7500 feet and about 8 inches in diameter will likely be the home of a badger. The marten, a relative of the badger, is a tan-colored tree climber the size of a small dog that snags its prey by sheer guile and quickness. Although extremely rare, the wolverine, a larger, ferocious relative of the badger, may still inhabit the more remote timberline areas of Shasta.

The mountain lion is also quite wary of people, but it undoubtedly still hunts on Shasta, for the authors have seen tracks near North Gate. Mountain lions prey chiefly on deer, and they no doubt move up and down the mountain with their prey. Black bears also live on Shasta, in the chaparral and forest zones. These animals are known to eat just about anything, but thankfully on Shasta they have not yet taken to raiding people's stores; the authors know of no instance on Shasta of bears getting into anyone's food.

9 The Geology

Most of us recognize that Mt. Shasta is a volcano, a "fire mountain" built by eruptions of seething hot rock from the interior of the earth. Indeed, Shasta is one of the largest of the many scores of volcanoes that ring the entire Pacific basin. These volcanoes are a result of the Pacific sea floor spreading east and west. At its margins the sea floor is forced to dive under the adjacent continents and into the earth's hot interior, where it melts. Part of this molten material works up to the surface to erupt and build a volcano.

The earliest eruptions in the Shasta area built the innocuous rise of Everitt Hill, just south of Shasta, about 500,000 years ago (y.a.). Eruptions that formed Mt. Shasta proper started between 400,000 and 300,000 y.a.. In geologic history this is quite recent, and the land that Shasta grew upon no doubt closely resembled its surroundings today.

By 300-250,000 y.a. there stood an early Mt. Shasta perhaps about as high as the present peak. We know very little about this proto-Shasta, for only a spiny, eroded segment remains of its original cone. This remnant forms the southeast side of Shasta, from Clear Creek to the east rim of Avalanche Gulch.

About 30,000 y.a. eruptions started to stack up a new cone, northwest of the original cone. Material from the new vent became what is now Casaval Ridge and most of the eastern flank of Shasta. A later eruption of this vent built up Misery Hill, the dark bane of climbers nearing the top of Shasta's most popular climbing route. About 9500 y.a. this vent's final gasp spilled forth the Red Banks, the brow of welded pumice that caps Avalanche Gulch.

About this same time, 10-9000 y.a., the vent that rapidly built Shastina opened up. Soon after, subsidiary vents on young Shastina's north flank poured forth lava flows that still look fresh today. Northeast of Weed,

Highway 97 takes a curving detour around the bluffs of what locals call "Lava Park."

Another striking feature of Shastina is the deep gash in its west face—Diller Canyon. Geologists aren't sure whether an inward collapse or an outward blast initiated this huge ravine, but in any case as Shastina grew it sent repeated eruptions of superheated rocks (pyroclastic flows) down it, scouring out the gulch and deeply burying the site of present-day Weed.

Shasta's most recent eruptions have stacked up a fourth cone, which makes up most of Shasta's northern flank and the summit area. One impressive legacy of this most recent vent is the Military Pass lava flow. Striking today even on a topo map, this flow poured down the canyon of Inconstance Creek to about 6100 feet, several thousand years ago. This vent continued erupting until just a few hundred years ago, and as testimony that it's not necessarily finished, a couple of small hot springs just west of Shasta's highest crags still hiss and bubble with sulfurous gases and water.

Like the eruptions of all the other Cascade volcanoes, Shasta's have varied in character, spewing out gas, molten lava, semimolten rocks, cinders (small particles) and ash (very fine particles) in various proportions. The products of the different eruptions cool to form different layers, or strata, of rock types, so Shasta is a *stratovolcano*. The major types of strata are lava and tuff. Lava is formed by a flow that is fluid and coherent, that spreads rather broadly, and that when cool forms blocky, fairly solid rock. Tuff results from semimolten ejected materials that settle together and congeal, often forming unstable cliffs. It's the interlayering of tuffs and lavas over the course of many eruptions that allows stratovolcanoes to stand so tall: tuff layers steepen the slopes and lava layers provide strength.

However, as one geologist put it, "Volcanoes can be thought of as ephemeral aggregations of unstable material." Recent studies of Shasta Valley, just northwest of Mt. Shasta, show just how unstable a volcano can be. Scores of hillocks and mounds pimple the terrain here; geologists now realize that these are eroded blocks of debris from a monstrous landslide off of the old proto-Mt. Shasta—the largest known landslide in the last million years. About 360-300,000 y.a. an estimated 26 cubic kilometers sloughed off the mountain, ran down the Shasta River plain past the present site of Yreka, and temporarily choked off the Klamath River. Although an earthquake or an eruption might have triggered the cataclysm, no evidence suggests this. The collapse might have been simply the fall of an oversteepened slope.

Hilly land of Shasta Valley--debris from ancient landslide

Smaller cataclysms have resulted when Shasta has erupted and melted glaciers and snow, as it often has. For instance, about 3000 years ago eruption-caused floods ran down Mud Creek Canyon, and the debris now underlies the town of McCloud and much of lower Squaw Valley beyond.

Neighboring Cones

Even a brief drive through the Shasta area reveals other volcanic vents. Most obvious is Black Butte, about 9500 years old, a steep cone that rises some 2400 feet above adjacent Interstate 5. Another, older cone is Ash Creek Butte, nine miles east-northeast of Mt. Shasta. Aligning more or less north and south of Shasta are the smaller buttes near North Gate, Red Butte, Gray Butte, McKenzie Butte and its satellites, and Everitt Hill. This pattern suggests an underlying north-south weakness in the earth's crust here.

Shasta's Glaciers

Glaciers form on high, cold mountains, where more snow accumulates during the winter than can melt during the summer. Over the decades the "excess" snow piles up and gradually compacts into ice. Eventually it gains enough weight to start creeping and flowing downhill. This river of ice rides down with almost irresistible force, pushing aside and grinding down rocks. Eventually the glacier's front reaches lower elevations where warmer climes melt it away. In this way a glacier is a gravity-driven system that dissipates "excess" snowfall.

Glaciers wax and wane with changes in the climate, and a persistent cooling of just a few degrees will bring on a glacial era. In a snowy but relatively warm climate like Shasta's, it's thought that cooler, cloudier summers are especially needed for glacier formation. The northern hemisphere seems to have been in such an era when Shasta first formed, so glaciers have no doubt periodically draped the mountain virtually since its inception.

Geologists can estimate the previous extent of glaciers partly by the characteristic mounds of debris, called *moraines*, that the ice rivers leave behind. Moraines around Shasta suggest that during at least one glacial period ice from the south slopes of Shasta merged with ice from Mt. Eddy and flowed to near the present site of Dunsmuir; to the north glaciers pooled in Shasta Valley; to the east Shasta's ice probably joined with glaciers from the Medicine Lake highlands.

The climate around Shasta has not always supported glaciers, however. At about the same time that Shastina was forming, a warm and dry period melted all permanent ice on the mountain. From 9000 to 3000 y.a., geologists think, there were at least a couple of glacial advances, but for much of this period Shasta probably held little or no ice. Starting about 3000 y.a. a cooler, wetter period brought on the "Little Ice Age," and fairly extensive glaciers accumulated on the mountain, probably even on its sunnier south slopes. This "neo-glaciation" continued strong into the late 1700s, and Shasta's present glaciers persist on a lesser scale from this time.

Today at least seven distinct glaciers flow down Mt. Shasta, including by far the largest ones in California. The Whitney Glacier is largest of all, pouring down between Shasta and Shastina, carving away at the flanks of both peaks. The Whitney shows a lot of *crevasses*, long cracks that formed when terrain underneath distorted the glacier's flow and generated tension in it. Snow can bridge these slots, sometimes thickly enough to obscure the gap but too thin to hold a climber's weight. To help keep from falling into these insidious traps, on snow-covered glaciers climbers use roped travel. The Whitney Glacier also spills over a couple of very steep sections, where the ice fractures into blocky, spectacular *icefalls*.

Mt. Shasta and Hotlum Glacier

Shasta's second largest glacier (in volume) is the Hotlum, which flows northeast from near the summit. The Hotlum also breaks into two or three icefalls. Relatively dry years since the 1920s have isolated a lobe of the Hotlum, and this has become known as the Chicago Glacier, for the annual studies conducted here by the University of Chicago.

The Wintun Glacier has a fairly active core section, which forms a small icefall as it drops into Ash Creek's upper canyon. The Bolam Glacier is extensive too, but its few crevasses and its gently sloping, receding terminus shows that it is relatively inactive.

Shasta's other three glaciers flow out of small, sheltered cirques in the mountain's southeast headwalls. The Konwakiton and Mud Creek glaciers (the latter is also called the Stuhl Glacier) spill out of small basins above Mud Creek; the Konwakiton is especially active and fractured for its small size. The recently recognized Watkins Glacier commemorates amateur geologist R.H. Watkins, who described this glacier and the post-1940 rejuvenation of Shasta's glaciers in general long before "official" geologists took notice.

The "neo-glaciation" gradually waned during the 19th century. At the turn of the century Shasta's glaciers briefly resurged, but soon after that a few warm, dry decades dramatically diminished them. The Wintun especially dwindled to just a vestige of stagnant ice. It wasn't until the 1940s that heavier snowfalls returned and rejuvenated the glaciers; for instance, by 1972 the Whitney had extended more than 1500 feet beyond its withered position of 1944. (Climatologists believe that the next few decades will be warmer and probably drier.

And in the longer term the "greenhouse effect" will probably bring even drier and warmer conditions.)

The wild fluctuations of northern California's climate in the 1980s have brought visible changes to Shasta's glaciers. The record winters of 1982 and 1983 started a "wave" of thicker ice moving down their lengths. Then the warmth of the drought years of 1986-88 melted away those gains, and no new snow accumulated, leaving very icy conditions for climbers on the north-side routes. The Bolam and Wintun glaciers, especially, appear thinner. References show that Whitney has thinned by perhaps 100 feet since 1983, although its terminus has continued to advance.

Hot summers occasionally cause Shasta's glaciers to release outburst floods. This happens when meltwater somehow pools up in a glacier, then bursts free. In 1924 Shasta's most infamous outburst flood gushed out of either the Konwakiton or the Mud Creek glacier, collected ice, mud and rocks on its way down between Mud Creek's unstable canyon walls, then rumbled beyond the mountain and damaged structures in McCloud. Silt from the flood choked off fish in the McCloud River and, some say, even clouded San Francisco Bay. Smaller outburst floods have raced down most of Shasta's canyons in this century—typically about once every 10 years—including some from the Whitney Glacier that in 1985 threatened homes north of Highway 97.

What everyone would like to know, of course is, "Will Mt. Shasta erupt again, and if so, when?" The geologic record gives every reason to believe that Mt. Shasta will erupt again, potentially destroying nearby towns. Imminent eruptions usually give enough warning for people to evacuate, but no one can now predict when such a future eruption might occur. During the last few millennia Mt. Shasta has erupted on the average every 250-300 years, and the last eruption may have occurred in 1786, which a French explorer apparently saw from his ship off the coast. From the late summer of 1978 through January 1981 periodic swarms of minor earthquakes shook the area, mostly centered east of Ash Creek Butte. These earthquakes were exactly the sort that indicate rising magma, but since then there has been only quiet.

10 Amenities, Sources and Other Information

Visitor's Information:

The towns at the foot of Mt. Shasta have a full range of supplies, services, food and lodging. You can obtain brochures and other useful information by writing or calling the Chamber of Commerce office in each town:

Mount Shasta; 300 Pine Street, Mount Shasta, CA 96067 (916) 926-4865

McCloud; 241 Main Street, McCloud, CA 96057 (916) 964-2471

Dunsmuir; 4841 Dunsmuir Ave., Dunsmuir, CA 96025 (916) 235-2177

Weed; 488 S. Weed Blvd, Weed, CA 96094 (916) 938-4624

Mt. Shasta is located within the Shasta-Trinity National Forest. The Forest Supervisor's office is at:

2400 Washington Ave., Redding, CA 96001 (916) 246-5222

Recorded recreational information: (916) 246-5338

There are two district ranger offices in charge of the Shasta area, one in McCloud and one in Mount Shasta. Maps, trail guides, campfire permits, campground information and various informative brochures are available at the offices. The Mt. Shasta Ranger District office maintains a complete visitor information facility. They also have an interpretive association retail outlet for a wide selection of books, maps, guides and even video tapes. A mail-order catalog is also available.

Mt. Shasta Ranger District

204 West Alma Street

Mount Shasta, CA 96067

(916) 926-4511

Recorded recreational information: (916) 926-3781

Office hours:

Winter (Nov. through April):Monday-Friday 8:00-4:30

Summer (May through Oct.):7 days per week 8:00-4:30

McCloud Ranger District
Minnesota Ave. and Highway 89
McCloud, CA 96057
(916) 964-2184
Office hours: 8:00-4:30

There are several professional guides and outfitters in the Shasta area who operate under permit from the U.S. Forest Service. Their activities include mountain climbing, ski touring, river rafting, fishing, pack trips and more. Several offer specialized trips for families, kids and the physically disabled, and continuing education courses in the legal and medical fields. You can obtain current listings of these outfitters, as well as brochures and information, from the district ranger offices.

The Mt. Shasta Ranger District maintains the following campgrounds:

Castle Lake	11 1/2 miles southwest of Mount Shasta on Castle Lake road.
Gumboot	15 miles southwest of Mount Shasta on South Fork road.
McBride Springs	4 1/2 miles northeast of Mount Shasta on Everitt Memorial Highway.
Panther Meadows	13 1/2 miles northeast of Mount Shasta on Everitt Memorial Highway.
Sims Flat	7 1/2 miles south of Castella off I-5.
Toad Lake	18 miles west of Mount Shasta off South Fork road, via Morgan Meadow road.

The McCloud Ranger District maintains the following campgrounds:

Ah-Di-Na	4 miles south of Lake McCloud off Highway 89.
Algoma	14 miles east of McCloud off Highway 89.
Cattle Camp	11 miles east of McCloud off Highway 89.
Fowler's Camp	6 1/2 miles east of McCloud off Highway 89.
Harris Springs	17 miles north of Bartle off Highway 89.

Other campgrounds include:
Castle Crags State Park
Castella, CA 96017
(916) 235-2684

There are two privately owned campgrounds both of which have excellent facilities. Lake Siskiyou Campground is located 3 miles west of Mount Shasta on the South Fork road. There are 299 campsites, and you'll also find showers, a store, a marina and a beach. There's excellent swimming in the lake, as well as boating, fishing and windsurfing.

Lake Siskiyou Campground
P.O. Box 276
Mount Shasta, CA 96067
(916) 926-2618

A spacious KOA campground is conveniently located at the north end of Mount Shasta city. There are 110 campsites and complete facilities.

KOA Campground
900 N. Mt. Shasta Blvd.
Mount Shasta, CA 96067
(916) 926-4029

Driving Tours:
The ranger offices have many free maps and information on driving tours to points of interest in the area. Two of the best trips are: Around Mt. Shasta via Military Pass Road, and the Seven Lakes Basin loop tour. Plan on a full day for each of these scenic jaunts.

Museum

The Sisson Museum, located on the grounds of the Mt. Shasta Fish Hatchery, is open year-round. Operated entirely by volunteers, the museum has many permanent displays on the history of Siskiyou County—particularly Mt. Shasta—as well as temporary shows that change several times a year. The hatchery itself is the oldest one in California. You will enjoy seeing the giant, docile brood trout swimming in their pools.

Location: Hatchery Lane and Old Stage Rd. (off Central I-5 exit), Mount Shasta, (916) 926-5508

Hours: Daily 10-5

Recreation

Shops in Mount Shasta that carry and rent outdoor equipment:

The Fifth Season
426 N. Mt. Shasta Blvd.
(916) 926-3606

The Fifth Season also has a 24-hour recorded phone message for the latest climbing and skiing conditions on the mountain: (916) 926-5555.

The House of Ski
1208 Everitt Memorial Highway
(916) 926-2359

The two above also rent ice axes, crampons and boots for climbing. Reserve in advance for holiday weekends.

The Sportsmen's Den
402 N. Mt. Shasta Blvd.
(916) 926-2295

The Mountain Shop
301 Chestnut St.
(916) 926-8650

Downhill Skiing:

Mt. Shasta Ski Park
The Ski Park is 10 miles from I-5 via Highway 89.
Office: 104 Siskiyou Ave.
Office: (916) 926-8600
Lodge: (916) 926-5254
Snow Phone: (916) 926-6101

Snow Play Area:

The Forest Service maintains a snow play area for sledding and sliding at Snowman's Hill, 6 miles east of I-5 on Highway 89.

Useful Information

Emergency

Fire, police, ambulance, highway patrol: Dial 911

Transportation

Amtrak 24-hour information:1-800 USA-RAIL
Greyhound Bus:(916) 926-2620
Holiday Travel Bureau:(916) 926-3491

Road and Weather

National Weather Service, 24-hour recorded message: (916)221-5613
Road Conditions, CHP, 24-hour: (916) 842-2716

Afterword

We're all guests, caretakers and cohabitants of this planet. As we move into the 21st century, environmental concern—and environmental degradation—has reached global proportions. Mt. Shasta, like many other unique micro-environments, shows man's impact.

Some common-sense guidelines apply to Mt. Shasta, as well as other wilderness areas:

- Be a thoughtful backcountry visitor. Know something about your route and the area, and follow the management guidelines of the governing agencies.

- Accept the responsibility of knowing the basics of first aid, navigation and minimum-impact camping.

- Choose your campsites thoughtfully, and leave them in as natural state as possible. Keep groups small and blend camps and tents into the environment.

- Even where a fire is possible, consider a fireless evening. Wildlands are feeling the effects of too many fires.

- Always use established latrines if they exist. If not, dispose of all human wastes appropriately: In winter, select a flat area away from rivulets, streams and creeks, to prevent the waste from entering a water source when the snow melts. Assuming the area is safe from fire hazard, carefully burn your toilet paper during the wet winter months.

- Do everything you can to protect water sources from contamination. Although giardia has not yet been reported on Mt. Shasta, its occurrence is increasing in the backcountry.

Index

Hiking in the backcountry entails unavoidable risk that every hiker assumes and must be aware of and respect. The fact that a trail is described in this book is not a representation that it will be safe for you. Trails vary greatly in difficulty and in the degree of conditioning and agility one needs to enjoy them safely. On some hikes routes may have changed or conditions may have deteriorated since the descriptions were written. Also trail conditions can change even from day to day, owing to weather and other factors. A trail that is safe on a dry day or for a highly conditioned, agile, properly equipped hiker may be completely unsafe for someone else or unsafe under adverse weather conditions.

You can minimize your risks on the trail by being knowledgeable, prepared and alert. There is not space in this book for a general treatise on safety in the mountains, but there are a number of good books and public courses on the subject and you should take advantage of them to increase your knowledge. Just as important, you should always be aware of your own limitations and of conditions existing when and where you are hiking. If conditions are dangerous, or if you are not prepared to deal with them safely, choose a different hike! It's better to have wasted a drive than to be the subject of a mountain rescue.

These warnings are not intended to scare you off the trails. Millions of people have safe and enjoyable hikes every year. However, one element of the beauty, freedom and excitement of the wilderness is the presence of risks that do not confront us at home. When you hike you assume those risks. They can be met safely, but only if you exercise your own independent judgment and common sense.

Acknowledgments

Without the help and support of many who love Mt. Shasta and associate themselves with the mountain, this book would have barely been possible. We'd like to especially thank geologists Dan Miller, Paul Dawson and Bruce Friend, botanist Dr. William Bridge Cooke, archaeologist and anthropologist Julie Krieger, meteorologist Jim De-Pree, Siskiyou County Deputy Sheriff Charlie Simpson, Lee Apperson and the Sisson Hatchery Museum, aerial photo expert Egon Harrasser, Tom Hesseldenz and the McCloud River Preserve, and the Bancroft Library.

Special thanks also to Jenny Coyle, Steven Labensart, Rick Poore, Phil Holecek, Kevin Lahey, Phil Rhodes, Steve Johnson, Nick Crane, Mark Rodell, Mark Duden, Larry Jordan, Perry Sims, and the folks at Fifth Season....

....all mountain people at heart.

—AS & MZ
Mount Shasta
June 1990